WORKBOOK

HIDING FROM LOVE

Resources by Henry Cloud and John Townsend

Boundaries
Boundaries Workbook
Boundaries audio
Boundaries video curriculum
Boundaries in Dating
Boundaries in Dating Workbook
Boundaries in Dating audio
Boundaries in Dating curriculum
Boundaries in Marriage
Boundaries in Marriage Workbook
Boundaries in Marriage audio
Boundaries with Kids
Boundaries with Kids Workbook
Boundaries with Kids audio
Changes That Heal (Cloud)
Changes That Heal Workbook (Cloud)
Changes That Heal audio (Cloud)
Hiding from Love (Townsend)
How People Grow
How People Grow audio
The Mom Factor
The Mom Factor Workbook
The Mom Factor audio
Raising Great Kids
Raising Great Kids for Parents of Preschoolers curriculum
Raising Great Kids Workbook for Parents of Preschoolers
Raising Great Kids Workbook for Parents of School-Age Children
Raising Great Kids Workbook for Parents of Teenagers
Raising Great Kids audio
Safe People
Safe People Workbook
Safe People audio
Twelve "Christian" Beliefs That Can Drive You Crazy

WORKBOOK

HIDING FROM LOVE

*How to Change the Withdrawal Patterns
That Isolate and Imprison You*

Dr. John Townsend
Coauthor of *Boundaries*

with *Lisa Guest*

ZONDERVAN™

GRAND RAPIDS, MICHIGAN 49530

ZONDERVAN™

Hiding from Love Workbook
Copyright © 2001 by John Townsend

Requests for information should be addressed to:

Zondervan, *Grand Rapids, Michigan 49530*

ISBN: 0-310-23828-5

Published in association with Yates & Greer, LLP, Literary Agent, Orange, CA.

Printed in the United States of America

01 02 03 04 05 06 07 08 /❖ DC/ 10 9 8 7 6 5 4 3 2 1

Contents

A Word of Welcome

The Bible continually proclaims our need for connection. God said it is not good for us to be alone (Genesis 2:18). At the deepest spiritual and emotional level, we are beings who need safety and a sense of belonging in our primary relationships with God and others. Yet, as one of the most destructive results of sin's entrance into the universe, each of us begins life in a terrified and disconnected state, making disconnectedness one of the most fundamental problems we can experience.

This disconnectedness is a violation of the very nature of God, of what he holds primary. God created us for a life of closeness and attachment. In fact, Jesus declared that the entirety of the Hebrew Scriptures rested on loving God and people (Matthew 22:37–40). One of the major causes of personal and spiritual struggles is that some part of the self is isolated from relationship. Such disconnectedness plays a large role in relational struggles, spiritual and emotional issues, and even work and career problems.

At some level, all of us have parts that are hidden and disconnected from God and others. This workbook is about helping you discover and bring before the grace of God and his people the wounded or undeveloped aspects of your soul that may have been in darkness. God himself and the body of Christ can mature, strengthen, and heal you as you enter his paths of life.

You will find that the three questions at the end of each chapter ("Coming Out of Hiding") are intended to help you both review the key points of the chapter and apply what you have learned.

May God bless your walk in him.

PART ONE
The Hiding Dilemma

Chapter One

Jenny's Story

Jenny's story is a fictional tale that illustrates the reality of hiding. We all hide in various ways. So, in this overview of Jenny's life, consider how you (or someone you know) may be a lot like Jenny.

Young Jenny's life was full of joy and comfort. She felt loved and secure until war broke out and her defeated country was occupied by enemy forces. Only a few days after the occupation, she saw several men crash through the front door of her home. "Run, Jenny! Run to the Deep Woods!" her father cried out. Looking back, Jenny saw the men drag her parents toward a big black car and shove them into the back seat.

- At first Jenny thought the occupying soldiers were friends. After all, they had military uniforms much like Officer Josef's police uniform. When has someone looked like a friend to you but eventually proved otherwise?

- When has someone cried out to you in warning (figuratively speaking), "Run to the Deep Woods"—or when have you chosen this option on your own? Briefly describe the dangerous circumstances you were leaving behind.

THE HAVEN OF THE DEEP WOODS (PAGE 18)*

The Deep Woods had always been Jenny's friend; now it was her only safe place. So she made the Woods her home.

* If you have settled into the Deep Woods, what memories remind you of a less isolated life?

* What fears and/or confusion keep you choosing to stay hidden in your Deep Woods?

LEARNING TO LIVE ALONE (PAGE 19)

Fear and loneliness became Jenny's constant companions. She hated being alone, but she was more afraid of exposure, especially to the men in uniform. The Woods were her safety; her memories kept her going as she made a place for herself in the forest.

* But something was different inside the little girl's heart. Her heart had been broken, and it did not mend while she was busy learning how to live in the forest. When, if ever, have you been aware of your heart—the part of you that once trusted and could make relational connections—becoming still and quiet, dull and painfully empty?

* What situations in life (if any) make you, like Jenny, feel inadequate to solve a problem or make a decision? Whose advice or past presence in your life offers you some encouragement or even direction in those situations?

*The page numbers in parentheses refer to the pages on which the corresponding sections are found in the *Hiding from Love* text.

- When is your aloneness in your own Deep Woods especially troublesome?

TERROR STRIKES AGAIN (PAGE 21)

When the four uniformed soldiers tried to catch her, Jenny plunged into deep, almost impenetrable brush. The soldiers ran right past her hidden path, and Jenny was safe.

- When, if ever, has your knowledge of your Deep Woods enabled you to protect yourself from further danger or harm? Be as specific as possible.

TROUBLING CONVERSATIONS (PAGE 22)

To make her day a little more interesting and a little less lonely, Jenny conjured up two imaginary friends: Big Jenny and Little Jenny. She repeated one of their conversations over and over again. It was a discussion of the very important question *Why am I here?*

- What conclusion is Little Jenny making about why she is in the Deep Woods?

- What, if anything, have you wrongly suggested to yourself about why you find yourself hiding in your Deep Woods?

ANOTHER CHASE (PAGE 23)

One afternoon another group of uniformed soldiers spotted Jenny and began running after her. Once again she escaped and hid too far away to hear them talk about their turning away the enemy and coming, according to her parents' wishes, to find Jenny and bring her home.

- Who might you have mistaken for an enemy—or who in your life right now might be a friend rather than an enemy?

- What similarities to past enemies (appearance, behavior) do you see in those who might be friends that keep you running and hiding from them?

JENNY'S SAFETY IN HIDING (PAGE 25)

By now Jenny had learned how to keep her life orderly and safe in the Deep Woods. She also noticed that, with each day, she felt less and less that she needed her old relationships. Emotions she had experienced before—love, tenderness, joy, and even terror, panic, rage, and sadness—were becoming more and more faint.

- Jenny's routine included all kinds of rules, even for little things. These rules helped give her a sense of control over her life. Does your life have lots of rules? Give a few examples.

- When, if ever, have you found strength in your sense of competency? In such a moment, what, if anything, have you noticed about your emotions or lack of emotions? What has happened (or is happening) to your heart as you have mastered surviving in the Deep Woods?

RESCUED FROM HIDING (PAGE 26)

On the twentieth day in a row, a uniformed man called out, "Jenny! Jenny! Where are you?" Still Jenny hid—until one day when he sat down and, for about an hour, called her name every few minutes. After Day 30, Jenny decided to take a small risk. She crept near the soldier, coughed to get his attention, and then vaguely recognized the face that turned toward her as her old friend Josef.

- Having come to take her home, Josef told Jenny that her parents had sent him to find her. When, if ever, have you felt, as Jenny did, the conflict between wanting to be in relationship again and being afraid to leave your Deep Woods? What did you choose—to leave the Woods or to stay?

- Who in your life, if anyone, might be able to lead you out of the Woods? What will it take you to, figuratively speaking, grab that person's hand just as Jenny grabbed Officer Josef's?

Coming Out of Hiding

1. Summarize what you have seen about how you and Jenny are similar. What hurtful experience led you into hiding? What places, behaviors, and habits have become your haven? What rules have you developed to give yourself a sense of control over your life? What changes in your perspective on the past and in your emotions have you noticed since going into hiding?

2. Think back to your own childhood and write down some of your memories. When were you happiest? What were you afraid of and why? Which relationships offered security? Which were tenuous? What did you learn about trust? Are you, today, needing to learn to trust again? What safe person (an "Officer Josef") might help you do that?

3. Spend a few minutes talking to God about how you, like Jenny, are hiding. This may be difficult if you are hiding from God. If that's the case, be honest about your struggle to pray and about how distant he seems. Ask God to be with you as you continue this study and to enable you to come out of hiding.

CHAPTER TWO

Our Two Biggest Problems

✤

D an left Sally. And when he did, he also left a question in her mind for a long time afterward: Why did Dan hide? What would possess him to conceal his heart from Sally, who would have cherished it? Why did he avoid the very closeness that he needed from a wife?

PEOPLE IN HIDING (PAGE 30)

For a variety of reasons, all of us live two lives: an external life, in which we learn the feelings, attitudes, and behaviors that are "safe" to express; and an internal life, in which we closet away our "unsafe" traits, which exist isolated and undeveloped.

- Our tendency is to keep the "unloved" parts of ourselves forever under wraps, with the hope that, in time, they will go away and not cause us more pain. What unloved traits do you keep under wraps? What pain are you reluctant to reveal? Why?

Jesus knows that we all have problems and needs, and he enables us to look at and resolve them through the resource of his understanding and love (Hebrews 4:15). But revealing these problems is often the larger problem. We call our efforts to conceal these problems *defenses*, a type of "fig leaf." We put up shields to keep ourselves from being exposed or hurt.

- We select our shields based on what injured part of ourselves we are protecting and who or what we are protecting ourselves from. When have you found yourself choosing compliance, withdrawal, and/or displacement as a defense? Be specific about the situations.

To understand what sends us into hiding, what compels us to build defenses, we must go back to foundational issues. I believe that the reason why we tend to hide our problems and struggles can be traced to two basic problems in life—which we will look at more closely now.

PROBLEM #1: WE'RE UNFINISHED (PAGE 32)

Our fundamental problem is that we are an unfinished people. As Christians, we are somewhat like a beautiful but damaged home under restoration.

- Like a mansion being renovated, we have a past of wonder and a future of hope. What is wondrous about your past? Start with Ephesians 1:4. And what is hopeful about your future? Begin with 1 John 3:2 and Ephesians 4:13.

- But what about the present? Like a mansion under construction, we are all in various stages of spiritual and emotional immaturity and disrepair. This period of being "under construction" can be a painful time of struggle (Romans 8:22–23). What loss, for instance, has your "under construction" period involved? What growth (if any) resulting from that loss are you aware of at this time?

THE UNFINISHED BUSINESS OF RELATIONSHIPS (PAGE 34)

The Bible proclaims our need for connection. It teaches that we are to form attachments with God: Jesus referred to our need to be close to him in his picture of the vine that nourishes the branches (John 15:4–5). The Bible also teaches that we are to form attachments with people (1 John 4:20). Our closeness to people is, to some extent, a measuring stick of our closeness to God.

- We are left with what may appear to be a simple formula. The problem is our need for attachment. The solution is to find intimate relationships. What about this simple formula is anything but easy for you? Why? What painful experiences or lack of experience of close involvement with others inhibits you?

We're unfinished people, and in many ways we hide from what we need to become finished and whole.

PROBLEM #2: WE FEAR WHAT WE NEED (PAGE 36)

Like the walletless man frantically looking in the wrong place for the right thing, we don't go to the right places to find healing for the broken parts of our souls. That's problem #2: Though we are an unfinished people, we fear and avoid the very things we need to restore us. We hide parts of our soul from love.

- Untangling the combination of "what's broken and why" is a major task we must undertake if we are to see the injured parts of our soul healed. At this point, what parts of your soul are you aware of being broken and in need of healing?

WHAT ABOUT ME? (PAGE 37)

You may be thinking that you really try to be open and honest and that your problem has more to do with relationships in which the other person is hiding. Consider these two points.

- First, hiding isn't always a process we are aware of. Sometimes our deep hurts and immaturities have been isolated from relationship for so long that we no longer have access to certain thoughts, feelings, or memories. Could that be a possibility for you? Yes or no, can you make the prayer of Psalm 139:23–24 your own? David's words there read:

  Search me, O God, and know my heart;
  test me and know my anxious thoughts.
  See if there is any offensive way in me,
  and lead me in the way everlasting.

- Second, different people hide different parts of the self. Some struggle with being open about their need to be loved. Others have difficulty bringing their more independent parts into the light. Think over the past few years of your life. Review the "regrets"—those relationships or opportunities you wish had turned out positively. Many of us can date our problems in important relationships to a point at which we began to conceal parts of ourselves from God, self, or others.

As I said in the introduction, this material deals with how we hide parts of ourselves from relationship, whether or not we are currently aware of doing so. I want to help you uncover and bring before the grace of God and his people the wounded aspects of yourself that have been in darkness. God himself and the body of Christ can heal your hurt places.

HOW DO I KNOW WHAT I'M HIDING? (PAGE 39)

How do we become aware of what is hidden? A scriptural teaching can help us here: the principle of roots and fruits. God has designed the universe so that we can identify problems based on their effects on our lives (Matthew 7:17–18).

- Results always point to causes. Our spiritual and emotional fruit points to our roots. Take a quick inventory of your current spiritual state and emotional health. What fruit, good and bad, do you see?

• Hiding always has some fruit, or symptom. The isolation of some part of our soul from love will always produce a problem. Symptoms can range from relational or family struggles to a failed marriage to depression, anxiety, guilt feelings, shame, eating disorders, substance abuse, career conflicts, physical ailments, and many others. Which items could you add to the fruits listed in response to the preceding question?

Awareness of our defenses is not all we need, however. No matter how much insight and information we have about our spiritual and emotional makeup, we require an environment of safe relationships to come out of hiding. This is God's design.

• This point can be missed in Christian circles, where it is often assumed that doctrinal exposure to the truths of the Bible, all by itself, is sufficient to ensure solutions to all problems. Yet Jesus himself stressed the need for relationship in order to take in truths. "I am the way and the truth and the life" (John 14:6) is one indication that knowing a person is necessary to knowing God's truth. When, if ever, have you felt pressure to let doctrinal teaching alone bring healing? What impact did this implicit expectation have on you and on the pain you were feeling?

We all have needs—that is, we all are unfinished. God has provided what we need to enter the healing and maturing process. Yet many of us feel spiritually and emotionally bankrupt, in pain, and unable to cope with life as we would like to. We are inherently unable to see what God has provided as good. It's as if he has laid out a banquet table for his children, inviting us to fill up, but something inside us sees danger in the invitation and causes us to turn away.

OUR DEEPEST ROOTS (PAGE 42)

To understand the roots of our two biggest problems—we are unfinished and we fear what we need—we have to go back to the very first story in the Bible. Adam and Eve planted those first roots that keep sprouting into hiding problems.

When Adam and Eve ate from the forbidden tree of the knowledge of good and evil, they gained experiential knowledge of evil, something we weren't meant to have. That's the essence of problem #1: a break in relationship with God, self, and others. Then, the story continues, Adam and Eve hid from God's restoring, forgiving, healing love (Genesis 3:7–10).

• We all can relate to the conflict of our original parents: we may have a "secret," which is either our own fault or our own shame, so frightening that it would be inconceivable to tell another about it. What fault or shame came to mind as you read that statement? If you can write it down here, you are taking a step away from hiding, a step toward God's healing light. If you are not ready to write it down or if nothing comes to mind, know that the purpose of this book is to help you come out of hiding.

• Our spiritual and emotional maturing is difficult enough in itself. And this difficult process is paralyzed when—because of past experiences, fears, shame, and pride—we withdraw from the very relationships and trust that would mature us. Our "fig leaves" keep us isolated from God, self, and others. The safety of the walls we built become a trap, as what was once a protection now becomes a prison. When have you seen someone (yourself or another person) imprisoned by behaviors and attitudes that were once a vital means of protection? Be specific.

The writer of Hebrews calls us out of our life in hiding: "Let us throw off everything that hinders and the sin that so easily entangles, and let us run with perseverance the race marked out for us" (12:1). Our subject is those encumbrances to our growth: where they come from, how they operate, what they tell us, and what we can do about them.

REMEMBER JENNY (PAGE 44)

Jenny represents all of us. She will appear at the end of each chapter, fleshing out the truths we are hearing. I hope that as you get to know Jenny, you will recognize your own hiding processes in her story.

- What behaviors, once needed for protection, kept Jenny imprisoned in the Woods long after the enemy soldiers had been defeated?

- What parts of your soul have you tried to keep safe from abandonment, ridicule, or injury? Don't worry if you can't answer this question now. After all, the purpose of this book is to help bring these to light, because these parts of you, which have remained disconnected, undeveloped, and unloved, need to be brought into relationship, connected, developed, and loved.

Coming Out of Hiding

1. We hide our problems and struggles because, first of all, we are unfinished and sinful people. In what ways does your life reflect an "unfinished" status? What brokenness are you afraid to expose? How have your efforts to hide your unfinished status and your brokenness interfered with your relationship with God? your relationships with other people?

2. Second, we hide from what we need to be whole—the love of God and relationships with his people—because we fear the very things we need. We withdraw from God, mistakenly seeing him as one who would hurt us. How similar to Adam and Eve's response to God after they sinned (Genesis 3:6–13) is your response to him after you sin? Explain. What keeps you from facing God with your problems as well as your sinfulness? What could God give you to help you move toward wholeness and holiness? What could his people give you to help you on that journey? Start making a list either of people who could be Officer Josef to you or of places you might go to find an Officer Josef.

3. Make David's prayer your own:

> *Search me, O God, and know my heart;*
> *test me and know my anxious thoughts.*
> *See if there is any offensive way in me,*
> *and lead me in the way everlasting.*
> —*Psalm 139:23–24*

Ask God to give you insight about your own "hidden parts" and a more accurate picture of who he is and what he wants to give you.

CHAPTER THREE

"This Wasn't in Plan A"

✛

Sherri had spent most of her life hiding her mistakes and failures from others. The "false self" she had created had finally taken its toll on her, and her feelings of burnout and depression were symptoms of the isolation and exhaustion she felt. As she explored her family background, she saw that failure had been a taboo topic in her family. She had learned to experience mistakes as painfully uncomfortable, something to avoid. Her family background had encouraged hiding, whereas the family of her husband, Bill, treated mistakes as part of life, something to learn from, definitely not something to fear or avoid.

- Are you more like Sherri or Bill in your attitude toward your mistakes and failures? Where did you learn either to hide your mistakes or accept your failures? Be specific.

THE WAY IT WAS SUPPOSED TO BE (PAGE 47)

God never intended hiding to be a part of our lives. It wasn't part of his own "Plan A." God's "Plan A" for us was a life of unbroken connectedness with him and one another. We were also to experience a deep, satisfying sense of purpose and accomplishment in performing the task he gave us. Our lives were meant to be filled with relationships and activity, or love and work.

- Our job description in Genesis 1:28 tells us to "subdue" the earth and "rule" over every living thing on it. The subduing function refers to the pioneering, groundbreaking tasks of life. The ruling function has more to do with running an already operating system. In what ways were you ever, or are you now, subduing and ruling? When, if ever, has doing so resulted in a sense of satisfaction and fulfillment? Be specific.

- "Plan A" called for us to learn, mature, and grow. Perfection doesn't exclude growth. *Perfection simply means that things are as they should be at a given stage of development.* What freedom to make mistakes does this definition of perfection give you? Why is that freedom important for someone coming out of hiding?

SINLESS IMMATURITY (PAGE 48)

Immaturity means that a goal has not yet been reached. Jesus himself experienced growing, practicing, and learning. The Scriptures tell us that he "grew in wisdom and stature, and in favor with God and men" (Luke 2:52). Jesus put himself through the same on-the-job training that we go through to learn about life, yet he did his learning and training without sin.

- What appeals to you about this definition of immaturity?

- Why is this perspective on immaturity helpful for someone coming out of hiding?

THE TWO TYPES OF GROWTH (PAGE 49)

It is important here to distinguish the two types of growth with which we constantly deal in the process of becoming mature Christians.

- ***Maturing Growth:*** In the maturing growth phase, we learn to develop those aspects of God's character he imparted to us (2 Corinthians 3:18).

- Maturing growth is moving from a good place to a better place. It is, for example, finding someone to care deeply about and finding our love deepening further or having a passion for a job and deepening our satisfaction in it. What example of maturing growth have you seen in someone's life or, ideally, experienced yourself?

- Many Christians lack patience with themselves or others in not being "instantly finished." If this is your struggle, what insight and even comfort or hope does the concept of "maturing growth" offer you?

- ***Restoring Growth:*** Restoring growth means that there is a problem; something is broken and needs fixing. We are unable to move out of our damaged position by ourselves. The brokenness is a result of a combination of our own sin (Romans 3:9–20, 23) and someone else's sin against us.

- Review the discussion of Jeremiah 17:9 and the example of child abuse found on page 52 of the text. In what ways has your own sin (your "deceitful" heart) caused you problems in life? And what hurts have you suffered, making your heart "desperately sick"?

- When have you blamed someone's emotional or spiritual struggles on that person's unconfessed sin—or when have you been confronted with that accusation? Why is such an accusation unfair and inaccurate?

- Optional: Why does pointing blame at the wounded person absolve the accuser of any responsibility for helping that person?

- When, if ever, have you experienced restoring growth? Be specific.

Jesus knows that we are an injured, as well as a sinful, people. Not all of our scars from the past are self-inflicted.

MATURING VERSUS RESTORING GROWTH (PAGE 52)

There is no qualitative difference between maturing growth and restoring growth. The only real difference between our normal spiritual growth and our growth out of damage is their relationship to time. Maturing growth is developing the undamaged aspects of the soul, while restoring growth concentrates on those parts that are damaged—that is, still lost in the past in an undeveloped state.

- Maturing growth deals with our "on schedule" parts. Restoring growth deals with our "behind schedule" parts. In light of this comparison, what growth do you need to do? If possible, give a specific example or two for each category.

God's process of spiritual growth is to reach into the soul, where the hurt parts of the person have been stuck in their injured places. With love, truth, and time, he helps bring those parts of the personality that are younger than the rest of the self back into sync with the whole.

- ***Growing in Both Ways:*** We need both types of growth. We need to keep maturing into the image of God in those areas in which we are undamaged. We also need to find and let God restore those aspects of our souls that are damaged, in a frozen state of immaturity, split off from relationship, and in need of restoring growth.

- Later chapters will help you get to know what parts of yourself need restoring growth. The prime place to start, however, is to notice what happens to you during times of stress or loss. What parts of your character begin malfunctioning under stress or in times of loss? Be as specific as possible. (You might also ask someone close to you to help you answer this question.)

— I withdraw from people.

— I caretake others.

— I cling to people.

— I become childlike.

— I become paralyzed.

— I become hysterical.

— I become all brain and no feelings.

— I eat.

— I stop eating.

— I use drugs or alcohol.

— I lose my temper.

— I crave _____.

— Other (name it):

HOLINESS VERSUS THE "SPLIT" (PAGE 54)

Many of us feel at times that some of our different parts—perhaps our feelings, our actions, or our thoughts—don't mesh together well. We need to remember that the goal of our growth process into Christlikeness is the integration of our character into a well-functioning whole. In Scripture the term *holiness* refers to believers being wholly devoted to and connected to God and detached from evil. *Holiness* describes a positive attachment to God and a refusal of whatever does not come from him.

• People whose injured parts have not been in the growth process never experience life as completely as they were designed to because something is not attached to the rest of themselves or to God. This kind of "split" is the opposite of holiness. Look again at page 55 of the text and the three main ways the term "splitting" is used in the *Hiding from Love* text. We all have split in the sense of the first definition. Where, if at all, do you see yourself in the second and third definitions?

• If you have a sense of your own hiding patterns, an awareness of ways you have been injured and ways you have stayed injured, you may not need professional help. In that case, in which of the following God-given resources for restoration do you think you are strongest? What will you do this week to draw from that resource?

— Close-knit relationships in local, growing churches

— Time in God's Word

— Thoughtful, fervent prayer for yourself and others

— Reliance on God's Spirit

— Exposure to helpful biblical teachers in areas of healing growth

AN ARMY WITHOUT AN ENEMY (PAGE 56)

Maturing growth was God's original plan. We were created to be learners and growers. We were meant to learn to receive and give love; we were meant to be active and productive. As we make mistakes, we learn. And hiding wasn't meant to be part of the practice process. Instead of causing us shame, errors we make while practicing should draw others closer to us. Our learning curve should bring us love.

- When, if ever, has your learning curve brought you love? Describe that experience—or its opposite: a time when making mistakes has brought shaming, condemnation, or even rejection.

- Whose learning curve have you not responded to in love? What can you do to ask forgiveness of God and of the person who made a mistake?

In "Plan A" there was no need for hiding. In fact, hiding would have been a little like having an army without an enemy. Before the Fall, in a world with no danger, we didn't need protection. Obviously, the situation has changed. In the next two chapters, we will deal with the needs we have that require protection.

REMEMBER JENNY

Jenny's memories of the safety of her family life helped her survive. Like Jenny, you and I need a safe place (a relational context), based on our heritage back in the Garden of Eden. God intends for all of us to be safe enough to grow. Part of all of us longs for that safety, when there was no need for hiding.

- According to the chapter's closing paragraph, what opportunity for restoration and reason for hope do Christians have?

- What have you learned (or been reminded of) already from this study about your own hiding patterns? about God? about his desire for your healing and growth?

- Briefly explain why, like Jenny, your memory of safety—your longing to not hide—can help you survive.

Coming Out of Hiding

1. Review the "Growing in Both Ways" question on pages 29–30. What clues, if any, does your response to those items give you as to the part(s) of you that need restoration? What injured part of your soul might be hiding behind these problems? Is it your ability to trust? to feel? to set limits? to be real? or something else?

2. Look again at the list of resources God provides his unfinished children. In which of these five resources do you believe you most need to grow? What specific step will you take toward tapping into that resource so that growth can happen?

3. Thank God for what he has shown you about yourself and about himself in chapter 3. Thank him for the maturing and restoring growth you have already experienced. Ask God to reveal to you what hurts and sins lie behind your typical responses to stress. Also ask the Lord to help you experience both the good and the bad of yourself. And ask him to show you what parts of you have split off. Listen quietly for what he might say to you. Finally, ask God to make his resources for restoration effective (or perhaps available) in your life.

CHAPTER FOUR

Our Need for Attachment

⁂

The Fall changed things for us. You and I live in a world that isn't as safe as when God first designed it. Yet it is not enough simply to understand that we need protection. We need to know what parts of our soul need protecting. Your soul is a remarkable creation of God, capable of great resiliency yet at the same time extremely fragile.

- Give an example of the great resiliency of the human soul.

- Now give an example of how extremely fragile the human soul is.

DEVELOPMENTAL NEEDS: OUR VULNERABLE PARTS (PAGE 60)

The best way to understand what parts of us we are to take care of is to look at our developmental needs. These needs prepare us for living and working in the world in an adult fashion. God has arranged these needs in definable stages of maturity that we are to grow through.

- Much of our spiritual growth occurs in stages. In fact, the Bible speaks of growth in identifiable steps that build one upon the other. As one is completed, we move to the next. Review the three steps outlined in 1 John 2:12–14 (discussed on page 60 of the text). At what stage do you think you are? What task is assigned to that stage and what are you doing to complete that task?

- Not only do we have different tasks for our differing stages, but also different ingredients to help us grow (Hebrews 5:12–14). In what areas of your life, if any, do you still seem to need milk? What could you do to grow through that "milk stage"?

As we work through the tasks required in each developmental stage, we progress to a new and deeper level of maturity that prepares us for the next.

OUR FIRST NEED: ATTACHMENT (PAGE 61)

Our ability to attach is our ability to relate our spiritual and emotional needs to others. To relate our needs to others is to connect or expose ourselves to them. Attachment means letting others inside the private, vulnerable parts of ourselves. Attachments occur when we take the risk to allow someone else to matter enough to us to hurt us if they choose to.

- How well are you able to attach to people? to God? If possible, give specific evidence of healthy attachment in your life.

Attachment is our deepest need, and it is the deepest part of the character of God. It is also the guiding law of God's universe. (Consider the complexity of the earth's ecosystem!) And, in the Bible, relationships or attachments are portrayed as crucial (John 15:4).

- Our need for connection extends not only to God; it also means we need each other (Ecclesiastes 4:9–11). When have you had a companion to lift you up when you fell or, conversely, when have you fallen and not had another to lift you up?

- Still considering the images from Ecclesiastes, when, if ever, have you been the companion to help lift someone up? What did this experience show you about why relationships (the giving aspect as well as the receiving aspect) are crucial?

ATTACHMENT AS A DEVELOPMENTAL NEED (PAGE 64)

Attachment is our primary developmental task. More than anything, we need to be drawn in to love, to be connected out of our aloneness. The beginning of life should offer a sense of welcome, transferred from parent to child, a feeling of "you belong with us; we're glad you're here; you're a part of this family." Ideally, parents devote the entire first year of their child's life to helping the infant take in, or internalize, this sense of belonging and safety. The goal of good attachment is *emotional object constancy*, the state of feeling connected even when one is alone. It comes as the result of constant reassurance by a primary caregiver. As love is taken in, it forms an emotional memory that soothes and comforts us in times of stress. Attachment deficits occur in different forms. But the common denominator is a lack of connectedness in the person's significant relationships.

- What insight does this discussion of attachment (found on pages 64–65 of the text) give you about some of the reasons why some people (maybe you yourself) may feel isolated and unattached to their world?

- Just as connectedness is our most basic need, isolation is our most injurious state. Isolation is serious because of the law of entropy operating in the spiritual world as well as the physical world. When have you seen (or perhaps experienced yourself) the spiritual and emotional entropy that comes with being isolated from God and/or other people? Describe the downward movement.

- Remember how Sheila was unable to ask for comfort for herself? Her life was devoid of relating to anyone other than on a "helper/helpee" basis. When Jesus called us to be like little children (Matthew 18:3–4), he was referring to the open humility that children possess in asking for their needs to be met. Are you like a little child in that sense? Support your answer with specific details from your life.

One more point about attachment: Since God created us for bonding, it is part of our very essence, just as it is in his essence. We cannot *not* bond. We are created to bond in either a growth-producing or a death-producing manner. Satan's plan is to help us get God-given, legitimate needs met in a way that will destroy us. John describes those counterfeits as "the cravings of sinful man, the lust of his eyes and the boasting of what he has and does" (1 John 2:16), or, as the King James Version puts it, "the lust of the flesh, and the lust of the eyes, and the pride of life."

- Who have you seen bond in a death-producing manner? Describe that person's situation. To what, if anything, have you bonded that is death producing in your life?

- Luke 12:34 reads, "For where your treasure is, there your heart will be also." Whatever is taking up emotional energy, money, and time is generally the bonding substitute. Which of the following attachment substitutes, if any, have you chosen?

Work	Sexuality
Sports	Shopping
Hobbies	Religious activities
Food	Knowledge/information
Parenting	Rescuing or "one-way" relationships

Put differently, what otherwise good things might you be using to keep away from the black hole of loneliness in your heart and the crucial necessity of close relationships? (Not-so-good substitutes include drugs and alcohol.)

The existence of emotional attachments in our lives—attachment to both God and human beings—is not an option; it is not a luxury. It is a spiritual and emotional necessity. God designed us for it!

HOW TO REPAIR ATTACHMENT DEFICITS (PAGE 69)

God's plan for repairing the unattached parts of ourselves is the story of redemption. God wants that isolated part of us to be brought out of darkness into the light of his love. Wherever the emotional object constancy process was interrupted, it must be continued until your heart is "caught up" with the rest of you.

• Do you know when your ability to bond was interrupted? Describe what happened to prematurely end the process and how old you were at the time.

• Repairing bonding deficits involves two factors. First, it requires finding safe, warm relationships in which emotional needs will be accepted and loved, not criticized and judged. Second, repair requires taking risks with your needs. Explain in your own words why these two steps are crucial.

Though relationship is what the soul needs most, it was relationship that injured it. An unbonded person can be devastated by further emotional abandonment. The risk of taking a healing step toward attachment involves the fragile aspect of the soul.

REMEMBER JENNY

When our unattached parts of the self become connected to others, our ability to tolerate loss of love from others increases. The more we internalize, the less we need the world to approve of us constantly. This is a hallmark of maturity. Loved people can feel loved even when their circumstances are emotionally dry.

- Remember what happened to Jenny's heart as she made a place for herself in the forest. Her need for attachment, like a muscle that is left alone, began to atrophy and wither. When, if ever, have you sensed your soul shriveling up due to lack of attachments to God and people? What did you do (or could you do) in that situation?

- Only with exercise will your attachment need grow and be properly reconstructed back toward the image of God that was defiled at the Fall. What workout program would you suggest for a person with a slightly atrophying attachment need? What specific need will you ask someone to help you meet? Whom will you ask and when? What will you do to move into closer relationship with God? With which Christian acquaintance or friend will you meet to share something about your loneliness?

Jenny experienced this atrophy in her aloneness. She felt brokenhearted, just as you and I do when we fall into hiding patterns within. We need to move toward relationship, toward attachment, to grow in Christlikeness. We need the emotional resources that God has provided: relationship with Christ and relationship with other image-bearers. We need to attach.

Coming Out of Hiding

1. Our ability to attach is our ability to expose our spiritual and emotional needs to others. It is our ability to say yes to relationship. On a scale from 1 ("No problem!") to 10 ("Impossible!"), how easy is it for you to let some carefully chosen others inside the private, vulnerable parts of you? Why do you think it is so difficult? Or why do you think it comes relatively easily?

2. Connection to God as well as to each other is necessary for survival (John 15:4; 1 Corinthians 12:26). Evaluate your connection to God. Are you able to abide in him, or are you still striving to be lord of your own life? Are you able to receive his gracious and unconditional love, or are you trying to earn a place in his kingdom? Is your relationship based on love for him or robotic compliance to his commands? Do you let him be your heavenly Father, or is he a distant, uncaring judge? Comment on why your relationship with God is like it is.

3. Jesus calls us to be like little children (Matthew 18:3–4)—to humbly acknowledge our needs and openly ask for them to be met rather than pretending to be self-sufficient. Right now confess your tendency toward self-sufficiency. Let your all-knowing, all-loving God know about your needs and about any isolation you may be feeling. Then ask him to be at work in you to heal the hurts (abandonment, abuse, detachment, superficial family intimacy, and so on) that have led to isolation. Finally, ask God to guide you to safe relationships with other people and to a more open relationship with him.

CHAPTER FIVE

Our Need for Separateness

❖

O ur need for attachment is our first developmental need, and Cathy illustrates our second. She understood her symptoms but not the problem. Cathy didn't have too much love—she had too few boundaries. She, like many Christians, had difficulty filtering out other people's needs from her own. Our second developmental need involves the quality of being separate, maturing our will, and setting boundaries.

- Are you at all like Cathy? Do you live with a sense of being overwhelmed by the demands of life? Do you experience problems in "keeping up" with all of your responsibilities? Do you tend to feel controlled by the needs and crises of others? Is it hard to filter out your own needs? If you answer yes to any of these questions, point to a specific time.

- What is your emotional response to the idea that we need to "be separate"? What might that reaction indicate?

WHAT ARE BOUNDARIES? (PAGE 74)

Boundaries tell us what is ours and—just as importantly—what isn't.

• People with poor boundaries find themselves continually taking on problems that aren't theirs and neglecting their own. After taking on everyone else's problems, they have no time for their own. Do you see yourself in this definition? Explain.

Boundaries are foundational to a sense of identity. They give us a clear sense of where "who I am" begins and ends.

• In what relationship, if any, have you lost a sense of where "who you are" begins and ends? What do you think contributed to that?

• Why are clearly defined boundaries essential for us to be able to love? Review the discussion on page 74 of the text and answer in your own words.

BOUNDARIES AND GOD (PAGE 74)

Much of the Bible is a portrait of God's character. When God describes himself, he does so in two ways: positively—what he is; and negatively—what he isn't. These "nots" are the boundaries of God; they are his method of letting us know him.

• Describe something about yourself by jotting down three or four things that you are.

- Now add three or four traits that you are *not*.

- Notice how easy this exercise was or wasn't. What might the difficulty, if any, tell you about yourself?

BOUNDARIES AND US (PAGE 75)

God has made us all stewards of certain things in our lives for which no one else can take responsibility.

- Consider those things over which you have stewardship: your time, money, feelings, opinions, thoughts, actions, values, gifts, and abilities. In what areas do you think God is pleased with your efforts? In what areas, if any, are you failing to take full responsibility?

Good stewards know what is not their responsibility. They know when a problem needs to be delegated, or isn't a high enough priority, or is simply someone else's.

- Look at your life from an outsider's perspective. (You might even want to ask a trusted friend about your tendencies.) Where, if at all, are you dealing with a problem with which you shouldn't be dealing?

- What do you do, or could you do, to try to distinguish life's better options from life's good options?

Next to bonding deficits, the problem of unclear boundaries is probably the most serious cause of emotional and spiritual struggles experienced by Christians today.

THE KNAPSACK AND THE BOULDER (PAGE 77)

Review the discussion of Galatians 6:1–5 (pages 77–78 of the text).

- The Greek word for "burden" in the second verse indicates an "overwhelming load," for example, those deep, catastrophic losses in our lives. What does God want us to do for someone being crushed by one of life's boulders?

- The Greek word for "load" in the fifth verse signifies "knapsack." A knapsack carries the essentials a hiker needs to make it through the day. It represents being responsible for ourselves—for our time, money, feelings, and the like. Which of these "supplies" are you not yet taking full responsibility for? And whose knapsack, if anyone's, are you trying to carry?

Taking responsibility for other people's feelings never works, because it deprives them of learning from the consequences of their behavior. Consequences are our teachers.

- When, if ever, have the consequences of your behavior (perhaps a mistake you made) taught you a lesson? Be specific about the behavior, the consequences, and even the lesson you learned.

- When, if ever, have you spared someone of the consequences of his or her behavior? Why did that seem like a good idea at the time? What course of action would you take now, after reading this brief section on boundaries?

BOUNDARY DEFICITS (PAGE 79)

People with healthy boundaries can say yes to the good and no to the bad. They are just as free to say no to someone they love as they are to say yes. That is because love is impossible without freedom. Love and fear cannot coexist, because fear removes the freedom not to love. Love entails free choice, not forced compliance.

- When, if ever, have you said yes to someone else's demands because you feared either hurting their feelings or provoking their emotional withdrawal? What were the consequences of that yes?

- When, if ever, have you said no to someone who is important to you? Was it hard to say no? Why or why not? If you can't think of a time you said no to someone you love, what does that suggest about your boundaries?

People who have been injured in their ability to set clear boundaries fall into two categories: those who take on others' knapsacks and ignore their own and those who need others to take their knapsacks.

- Which category, if either, do you (or someone you know) fall into?

- If you see yourself as overresponsible, when, if ever, have you sought a needy, dependent person? If you found one, describe that relationship.

- If you see yourself as underresponsible, when, if ever, have you sought a caretaker? If you found one, describe that relationship.

- In which, if any, of the following additional indicators of unclear boundaries do you see yourself? Give specific examples.

  — Making commitments under pressure that you never would make with a clear head

  — "Caving in" to others

  — Struggling to speak your mind

  — Afraid to be honest and tell the truth

  — Unable to protect yourself in injurious situations

  — Unable to stand firm and separate with your own values

  — Lack of direction in life

Whatever you are not aware of, you can't repair. But if you have identified a pattern in your life, you can now take responsibility for it and choose a healthier path.

HOW TO REPAIR SEPARATENESS DEFICITS (PAGE 81)

No one has perfect boundaries; at times we all take on what is not ours or don't take on what is ours. To improve your boundaries, whatever condition they are in, consider the five steps outlined on pages 81–83 of the text.

1. Ask God to help you become a truth-teller, even of negative truths.

    — With whom will you practice telling the truth?

    — From whom, if anyone, are you concealing your anger? Why is admitting anger important to repairing separateness deficits?

    — What would be an appropriate response when someone shares with you that he or she is angry with you? In what ways do you want to respond to negative truths?

2. Find people who celebrate your separateness.

    — Whom do you know who is "for" you being separate? Spend time with that person. (Or where can you go to find such a person?)

— When, if ever, have you chosen to be in a bad relationship rather than in no relationship? Why (if you can figure it out) did you stay— or are you staying?

— Think of two or three people to whom you are close. Do you love their no as much as you love their yes? Are you affirming compliance and withdrawing from them if you disagree? If you aren't loving someone's no, you aren't loving that person.

3. Practice disagreement.
   — Why does it make sense that you will rock some boats as you begin to set boundaries?

   — How do you want to respond to legitimate disagreement?

4. Take responsibility for your mistakes.
   — Why do many people choose blaming or rationalizing rather than taking responsibility for their mistakes?

— Learn to admit when your problems are the result of your irrespon-sibility rather than finding excuses. The excuser has nothing to fix. In light of that statement, how do you want to handle the mistakes you make?

5. Learn to respect others' separateness.
   — Who in your life, if anyone, do you have on a pedestal? Explain why learning to accept another's boundaries keeps us from idolizing that person.

   — If we want others to accept our freedom, we must respect theirs. How will you react to another's no—clear evidence of that person's separateness?

• Which of the five steps you just reviewed will you focus on this week? What will that focus look like in terms of actions and attitudes?

A FINAL NOTE (PAGE 84)

People with fragile boundaries have a harder time loving because of their lack of freedom. The most loving people in the world have a clear sense of their separateness and stewardship of themselves.

- Jenny had a very healthy separateness that helped her survive her separation from her parents. She also had clear boundaries, and she knew when they were being violated. How similar to Jenny are you? How do you deal with periods of loneliness? Could you survive the sort of experience Jenny had with the same sort of responsible stewardship? Why or why not? Be specific.

- Our souls need both bonding and belonging in order to build relationship and to function in life. In which area do you need to do some work? Explain why you answered as you did.

Our ability to bond deeply with God and others and our ability to take biblical responsibility for ourselves determines much of the quality and meaningfulness of our adult lives. So does a third developmental need—the ability to accept the presence of good and bad in the world and in ourselves. We will look at this in the next chapter.

Coming Out of Hiding

1. Our second developmental need involves the quality of being separate, maturing our will, and setting boundaries. It is our ability to say no, to perceive what is our responsibility and what is not. On a scale from 1 ("No problem!") to 10 ("Impossible!"), how easy is it for you to set boundaries? Do you do a good job taking care of yourself, or are you more concerned about pleasing people? Why do you think setting boundaries and letting yourself be separate is either relatively difficult or easy for you?

2. The boundaries we set with other people are an issue of stewardship (2 Corinthians 5:10). Over what things in your life has God made you a steward? Put differently, what things are in your knapsack? For what things in your life can and should you (not someone else) take responsibility? Second, for what people and situations in your life are you taking responsibility even though they are not your responsibility? Whose knapsack are you carrying? Why?

3. In response to Paul's words in Galatians 6:1–5, ask God to help you recognize the knapsacks and boulders in your life. Ask him to help you release knapsack items that aren't yours, to carry your own knapsack responsibly, to receive the help he wants to give you through his people, and to enable you to help in a healthy way those people you know who are themselves bearing burdens. Also ask God to help you with the boundary skill (numbers 1–5 in "How to Repair Separateness Deficits") you are working on this week and to bring healing to those parts of your soul that make setting, keeping, and honoring other people's boundaries so difficult.

CHAPTER SIX

Our Need for Resolving Good and Bad

✛

C arol's deep sense of disappointment with her two former husbands and her various careers led to a sense of resentment toward God for "not being fair" to her. In her early forties, she was no closer to the ideal life than when she was younger. Carol's hope had moved to despair (Proverbs 13:12).

THE CLASH OF REAL AND IDEAL (PAGE 88)

Carol's conflict illustrates our third developmental need: We must learn to live with the tension of a fallen world, of knowing that the universe, like us, is sinful, marred, and imperfect.

- When has the tension between the real and the ideal been most obvious and/or distressing to you? Describe the situation, what brought this tension into focus, and how you responded emotionally.

- We human beings have an idea of what the ideal, perfect world would be. The contrast between it and our current world is brutally difficult to swallow. Give two or three examples of how the world today is hardly ideal. The front page of the newspaper might serve as a good starting point.

God never wanted us to be able to make moral judgments of good and evil. The reason seems to be simply because he wanted to spare us the experience of evil. The knowledge of evil is so contaminating that God alone can deal with it without becoming evil himself. Our creatureliness makes us susceptible to its power.

- Review the discussion of the Fall on pages 89–90 of the text. What insight was new and/or especially helpful? List one or two points.

The experience of imperfection and the knowledge of good and evil—Adam and Eve's legacy to us—land a one-two punch on us, and a dilemma is born. It can be stated this way: "I'd like to be the ideal me—living in an ideal world. I can even imagine it. What then do I do with the badness in myself and in the world? How do I coexist with injustice? failure? imperfection? disappointment?"

- When, if ever, have you encountered this dilemma? Describe the situation. Or, if it is a familiar voice and regular presence with you, suggest its source.

- Behind this dilemma caused by imagining the ideal but living with very real badness (experienced most intensely by the perfectionist or frustrated idealist) is a fear that bad will overwhelm and contaminate good. This is a sign of a developmental inability to trust that the good can coexist with the bad. Would you describe yourself as a perfectionist or frustrated idealist? Why or why not? Next comment on your ability or inability to trust that good can coexist with bad.

Carol, the woman who was chasing the "ideal" husband, family, and job, was unable to accept mediocrity and flaws in her life. She embarked on a life-long journey to the land of Oz, where she would never have to be disappointed again. Good enough wasn't good enough for Carol's idealistic dream.

A DEVELOPMENTAL VIEW (PAGE 91)

Infants experience the same difficulty Carol struggled with (pages 91–92 of the text), and the apostle Paul suffered greatly with the reality that sin lived within him (Romans 7:15–19).

- What insight into infancy and early childhood did you gain from this discussion? What insight into yourself, if any, did you gain?

- Paul said, "What I do is not the good I want to do; no, the evil I do not want to do—this I keep on doing" (Romans 7:19). What about yourself comes to mind as you read those words?

Paul felt the internal conflict—the alienation—the destructive splitting between his goodness and badness, knowing who he should have been and yet also who he really was. And it is a conflict with which you yourself may be all too familiar.

FALSE SOLUTIONS (PAGE 92)

People who have not received enough grace to solve the badness problem are constantly on the run from the shame of their own sin or the disappointment of seeing the badness of others—or both. Temporary and therefore false solutions involve some sort of splitting between good and bad, keeping the two apart rather than realistically resolving them through forgiveness from God and others.

- A typical temporary solution is intolerance of our own badness. (Remember Jeff's story [pages 93–94 of the text]?) Fixating on goodness—while ignoring badness—can lead to an addiction to self-admiration. It leads away from love. Love sees—and forgives—the bad (1 Corinthians 13:6). Love doesn't deny the truth, positive or negative. Describe your attitude toward your badness. In what ways, if any, are you keeping your badness in a secret compartment away from the rest of your life?

- A second false or temporary solution to resolving the tension between good and bad is the problem of intolerance of the badness in others. This was Carol's situation (pages 95–96 of the text), so she retreated into a fantasy world. But her constant state of gracelessness, or her feelings of unlovableness and badness, made her hypersensitive to other people's remarks. She would easily feel wounded or misunderstood. To what degree, if at all, are you like Carol, either in constructing a fantasy world or being hypersensitive to how people treat you? Give evidence from your life.

Often, denial is the only way people learn how to deal with the unpleasant aspects of their souls. Splitting off the feelings, thoughts, or memories from awareness helps ease the unloved feelings and shame. The only problem is that *denial doesn't work*. Parts of us that are buried are always buried alive.

THE BIBLICAL SOLUTION (PAGE 96)

Since none of us is as "graced" and secure as we could be, all of us need help in solving the tension of what to do with our bad parts. God's solution is not perfectionism or splitting off our badness. It is quite the opposite. It is called *forgiveness*.

- *Love Versus Law:* Biblically, the antidote to the badness in our hearts and in the world isn't our goodness. That would be legalism or self-salvation. But Jesus' death took morality problems out of the arena of *law* and into the arena of *love*. The message of the Bible is that our exposed parts are exposed to relationship so that we can be cared for, forgiven, and supported. This happens through the process the Bible calls *confession*.

— The Bible teaches that all have sinned and fallen short of the glory of God (Romans 3:23). What is freeing about this? And why does this make Jesus' death on the cross even more remarkable? See Romans 5:8.

— On a scale from 1 ("Not even on the radar screen") to 10 ("'Terrified' is an understatement!"), how concerned are you about having your weaknesses exposed and shame, rejection, and isolation from God and people heaped upon you? In what ways, if any, are you either trying to make up for your imperfections or denying them?

• **_Confession:_** To confess means _to agree with the truth about ourselves._ If this truth is a secret compulsion, a shameful memory, or an unloved self, we are to agree about it with God and other people (James 5:16). Rather than being a path to condemnation, confession to God and others is a gateway to solving the problem. Being realistic and vulnerable leads to healing.

— The purpose of confession is to bring the unloved, hated, bad parts of ourselves into both the light of God's grace and the clear direction and instruction of his truth. Love reduces our badness to its essence: our bad part is simply a problem in getting our needs met biblically. To whom could you bring your bad parts—or where might you go to find a safe friend, confidant, counselor, or pastor?

— When, if ever, have you experienced something of the relief and healing that confession brings? Let revisiting that experience encourage you to confess again. If you don't know the healing power of confession, ask God to provide you with both the courage and the opportunity to take that important step.

Like Jeff, you can integrate your "bad" aspects into the rest of your character, take responsibility for them, and be accountable to have them loved and understood by others. And confession is key to the process.

HOW TO ATTACH THE BAD TO RELATIONSHIP (PAGE 98)

Grace is about not being afraid of imperfect things in ourselves or others because there is always more grace than badness. If imperfection is a large landmass in our lives, grace is an ocean that can swallow it up. Badness will never compete with grace. It's not in the same league.

- Granny validated a part of me (my long hair) that had been troublesome in my life. When she did, something that had been broken in me began healing. When, if ever, has someone given you the opportunity to respond with grace to his or her badness? Reflect on that situation.

- Who in your life, if anyone, might offer grace to you if you confessed your "bad" or imperfect parts? Or, again, where might you go to find that kind of person?

As the negative parts of our soul are confessed and attached to loving, accepting relationships, we learn to deal with them honestly and without fear. Because in those relationships there is no threat of impending rejection, we can feel safe discussing, exploring, and confessing these bad parts.

- Review the skills (listed here) that can help you resolve your good/bad split (pages 99–100 of the text). Which skill is the most challenging to you? Which is the most urgent? What step will you take this week toward developing one or both of the skills you just identified?

  — Confess your lacks to God and people.
  — Receive forgiveness.
  — Let go of the demand for the ideal.
  — Accept "good enough" in yourself and others.
  — Make sadness your ally instead of your enemy.

TWO BADNESSES: A FINAL NOTE (PAGE 101)

It is important to recognize the two types of badness.

- The first is the actual sinful, depraved part of our souls (Romans 3:12–17). It is a movement away from meeting our needs in God's way and toward meeting them in Satan's counterfeit way. What kinds of this first badness—what specific sins—would you do well to confess right now? Take several minutes to confess where you are not meeting your needs God's way.

- The second type of badness is perceived badness. It may or may not be an actual sinful aspect of the self. It is, however, experienced as bad. When others withdraw from us because of certain traits we have, we see those parts of ourselves as bad. Examples include our needs, our anger, our will, our anxiety, our sadness, and even our exhilaration. Terri was taught that needs—real emotional needs, not wants or desires—were bad. What personality trait(s), if any, have you been taught to think of as bad?

The resolution of both badnesses is similar. Both our actual and perceived bad aspects of personality need confession and relationship. Both need to be accepted as part of the self. The only essential difference is this: while actual badness requires repentance and humility, the focus of perceived badness is more on experiencing the truth about ourselves in relationship.

REMEMBER JENNY

Jenny was forced to deal with good and bad men in uniform. She learned to hide from invading enemy soldiers. Later, however, when soldiers from her own country's army came, she ran from them as well. The problem was that Jenny had not resolved the difference between the two kinds of soldiers. Her *perception* of the soldiers caused her to run away the second time.

- Like Jenny, we sometimes go into hiding because we have not resolved what is good and bad in our lives. Is this the case with you? Are there incidents in your past that haunt you and cause you to perceive others as "bad" when they aren't necessarily so? Or do you have certain personal traits that you have decided are "bad"—but this impression has been formed largely because of unpleasant experiences with others? Or perhaps you have never come to grips with your own nature—in which case it may be helpful to consider seriously the claims of Christ and his offer of forgiveness through the cross.

In any of the cases just listed, serious reflection on your goodness and badness is necessary. Your humanness possesses both, and resolving the split is one of your most important tasks in maturing. So is the issue addressed in the next chapter, our need for authority and adulthood.

Coming Out of Hiding

1. Our third developmental need is learning to live with the tension of a fallen world, accepting that the universe (like us) is sinful, marred, and imperfect. We need to come to trust that the good can coexist with the bad. On a scale from 1 ("No problem!") to 10 ("Impossible!"), how well do you cope with the world's imperfections? other people's imperfections? your own imperfections? When has "good enough" not been good enough for you?

2. God's solution for dealing with our badness is not perfectionism or works (Romans 11:6), but confession (James 5:16) and forgiveness (1 John 1:9). Look again at the five skills that can help you resolve your good/bad split (pages 99–100 of the text). Choose one to focus on this week and come up with a specific plan of action.

   Skill 1: When will you spend some time with the Lord confessing your sin? With whom will you meet to admit your imperfections?

59

OUR NEED FOR RESOLVING GOOD AND BAD

Skill 2: Let yourself receive forgiveness from the person to whom you admit your imperfections—and from God himself.

Skill 3: What ideals-turned-demands do you need to let go of? Make a list.

Skill 4: What aspects of yourself, your relationships, your job, and so on, can you start accepting as "good enough"?

Skill 5: What losses do you need to spend some time processing? What situations do you need to let yourself feel bad about?

3. Ask God to guide you as you work on the issues of chapter 6. Ask him to help you distinguish between actual and perceived bad aspects of your soul and your personality; to help you take responsibility for actual badness and learn from its consequences; to free you from perceived badness; and to forgive yourself and others for failures, weaknesses, and sins.

CHAPTER SEVEN

Our Need for Authority and Adulthood

✤

People in positions above Phil loved his compliance. All those below him felt beat up by his control. All of Phil's work relationships were uneven: either one-up or one-down. His situation introduces our fourth developmental need in restoring the image of God in us: coming into adulthood and taking on appropriate authority roles. Authority has to do with the following issues: personal power, expertise, responsibility, appropriate submission, sexuality, and the ability to think independently. Properly developed, these are the character traits of a mature adult.

A BIBLICAL VIEW (PAGE 106)

To understand the proper place and importance of authority, we need to look at God. God is king. He rules over the universe (1 Chronicles 29:12). Yet, like any good chief executive, God is a delegator. He confers power on others to carry out his plans. Adam and Eve were delegated authority to rule the earth (Genesis 1:28), but their rebellion against God removed rulership from their hands, and God's creation began moving away from his rule.

- What evidence of God's creation moving away from his rule do you see in the world around you today?

- Instead of being authorities over the earth in God's image, we became slaves to sin. Instead of reigning over the planet, we experienced sin's reign over us. What evidence of sin's reign over humanity in general do you see as you look around?

The representatives of the King became prisoners. And this is the motivation behind the coming of Christ. His death freed us from bondage to eternal isolation and darkness (Romans 6:18). The Son, under the authority of the Father, gave us freedom to be reestablished as image-bearers to work again in the role of subduing and ruling.

- What evidence do you see that God is reclaiming his territory through redeemed lives, through Christians who live out their faith in their marriages, families, neighborhoods, and workplaces?

- Knowing how to respond to—and become—an authority helps us with the task of discharging our God-given responsibilities. List some areas where God has given you responsibility. How does God the King expect you to exercise your authority in those areas? See, for instance, Proverbs 22:29, Matthew 6:33, Ephesians 4:25, and Hebrews 12:12–13.

The day will come when God's rule is again complete. In the meantime, we are to rule wisely under our Wise Ruler. That is why learning to exercise the authority we have over our lives today is so important.

A DEVELOPMENTAL VIEW (PAGE 109)

The family, as a creation of God, has a central purpose: to develop adults who can continue the subordinating of the earth to the kingdom of God. The successful family moves its children gradually to the place where they can take charge of their lives.

- From birth till puberty, much of parenting is a matter of love and limits. Comment on the balance maintained by your parents and, if you are a parent, the balance you are maintaining. If 1 is permissive and 10 is authoritarian, where do the two homes fall on a scale from 1 to 10? Explain.

- From puberty until leaving home, the parent's job changes from controlling the children's behavior to helping them stand on their own. This still involves rules and limits, but now those guidelines must be more flexible and negotiated. Again, consider the parenting you received and the parenting you may be exercising. What did your parents do well? What is most challenging to you as you parent your teenagers?

- Explain in your own words why it is important for teens to push away their parents and to question things (including what their parents are doing and why).

This fourth developmental stage is the culmination of the first three. The family first teaches the child to attach. Next, it trains her to be separate—to set boundaries and respect the boundaries of others. Third, it provides a place where she can deal with good and bad in herself and the world. And, finally, it reinforces the abilities and strengths of the maturing person as it helps her take her place in the world.

THE MEANING OF AUTHORITY (PAGE 111)

Besides "power" and "dominion," *authority* also means "expertise." God's plan for our maturity is that we become an expert in something. The expertise entailed by authority is God's way for the body of Christ to operate in an interdependent way.

- What have you become an expert in?

- How has this expertise helped you enter into the adult world and be connected with other people?

Authority means looking at the meaning behind rules, not simply at the rules themselves. Rules are to be the servants of love. As Jesus taught, when a tradition prevents love or hurts the innocent, it needs to be broken in the name of love (Matthew 12:1–7, 10–13).

- Rule-bound people who have a controlling edge would rather be right than loving. For them, correctness is a matter of action, not of relationship. In what ways, if any, did your parents—or do you—esteem correctness over relationship? Give a specific example or two of either correctness or relationship taking precedence.

Looking at the meaning behind the rules gives love a chance to win out.

SEPARATENESS VERSUS AUTHORITY (PAGE 112)

It is easy to mistake the stage of authority and adulthood for the stage of separateness and boundaries. Both involve the development of more aggressive functions in us, more confrontation, and more "pushing." But the stages are fundamentally different.

- Boundaries result in the existence of a separate person. Authority results in our introduction into the world as a functioning, mature adult. Why does it make sense that the stage of separateness and boundaries precedes the stage of authority and adulthood? Put simply, why is separateness essential to adulthood?

- Many people with solid boundaries have no clue about how to hone special abilities or develop career goals, about how to handle sexuality, or about how to take their place of authority in the world. In light of these criteria, evaluate your own level of maturity. Where do you see opportunities for growth?

Many people feel like a child in a grown-up world. They have not felt permission to become an adult.

HOW TO REPAIR ADULTHOOD (PAGE 113)

Resolving the problem of feeling like a frightened or enraged child in a grown-up world is a crucial developmental task. We must move from feeling one-down or one-up to others, to taking responsibility for developing our own position in the world as an adult. Accomplishing this task requires several skills.

- Review the list of skills below that can help you step into a position of authority and adulthood according to God's design (pages 113–16 of the text). Which skill is the most challenging to you? Which is the most urgent? What step will you take this week toward developing one or both of the skills you identified?

  — Question authority and learn not to idealize, but to accept the good and the bad.

  — As you question, also submit to appropriate authority (Romans 13:1; Hebrews 13:17), seeing authority as positional rather than personal and remembering that authority has its parameters.

  — Take an inventory of your values and convictions, noting both what you believe and why.

  — Address adults as adults, not parents.

  — Develop your talents—and that may mean pursuing something very different from your family's expectations.

— Make sexuality a good thing. A relationship in which sexually frank discussions can take place among mature adults can help.

— See guilt as a sign of growth, a sign of taking risks, and, often, of showing us that we are attempting to become adults.

SUMMARY (PAGE 116)

In these last four chapters, we have looked at the building blocks of character in the image of God:

The ability to be attached and to attach.

The ability to be separate and set boundaries.

The ability to live with the good and bad of ourselves and others.

The ability to establish oneself as an adult with appropriate adult authority.

God's plan is for us to fully develop all four of these aspects of our personality. The problem is that we all are injured at some level.

• When our growth is arrested in the development of these parts, we remove ourselves from further growth. By hiding, we try to protect ourselves from further pain. And sometimes we bury certain aspects of our soul so deeply that we lose awareness of their existence. When, if ever, have you noticed in yourself a tendency to protect yourself? Which of the four aspects of your soul were involved? What kind of pain were you trying to avoid and what was your strategy?

- The frozen aspects of our souls desperately need the light of grace and the instruction of truth. But we are terrified that we will experience even more isolation, hate, or criticism than we have already felt. This doesn't make all hiding bad. Some self-protections are necessary for spiritual and emotional growth. When, if ever, have you seen in yourself or someone close to you some necessary self-protection? Why was it necessary? What kind of self-protection was involved? Was it successful? Why or why not?

REMEMBER JENNY

Jenny struggled with the adult decisions thrust on her by her hideout in the Woods. Her authority need was great, but she was developmentally incapable of such maturity. Jenny developed a helpful inner hiding pattern: she would recall Officer Josef's wisdom to help her deal with the challenges she faced. Her conversations between Big Jenny and Little Jenny, however, were a harmful hiding pattern.

- Think about your own struggle for adulthood. What painful memories, if any, have hindered your ability to function as an adult?

- Ask yourself some hard questions about your abilities in the seven skill areas listed in the "Summary." In which areas do you need to grow? In what areas would you like to grow? What would such growth mean for your adulthood?

In the next five chapters, we will look at how hiding can sometimes be helpful and other times be harmful. It is important that we recognize these patterns in order to become healthy and fully functioning adults.

Coming Out of Hiding

1. Our fourth developmental need involves coming into adulthood, taking on appropriate authority roles, and managing our lives as functioning, mature adults. We need to learn how to respond to authority as well as to take authority whenever appropriate. Authority has to do with such issues as personal power, expertise, responsibility, appropriate submission, sexuality, and the ability to think independently. Which of these areas are points of struggle for you? Where in your family, your church, and/or your work do you struggle to respond to authority and/or to take authority?

2. Look again at the seven skills suggested for resolving the problem of feeling like a frightened or enraged child in a grown-up world (pages 113–16 of the text). Choose one to focus on this week and come up with a specific plan of action.

   Skill 1: Which spiritual, financial, relational, or career leader will you let yourself disagree with and/or ask questions of?

   Skill 2: Evaluate your submission to those in authority over you. Is your submission healthy or extreme? appropriate or absent? What would God say to you about how to act in these situations where you find yourself under another's authority?

   Skill 3: Do a personal faith evaluation. Ask yourself, "What do I believe about God? Jesus Christ? salvation? the Bible?" Then find out why you believe what you believe.

   Skill 4: With whom do you relate from a one-down position? What will you do differently the next time you are with him or her? Consider such things as making eye contact, adjusting your vocabulary, and using first names.

Skill 5: What interest or talent could you start developing? What goals do you want to reach? If these two questions are hard to answer, what will you do to get to know yourself better?

Skill 6: With whom can you have a frank discussion about sex? What specific aspects of your sexuality do you need to normalize as "something adults do"?

Skill 7: What actions and thoughts that prompt feelings of guilt may, in fact, be signs of your growth toward adulthood?

3. Summarize your competence and comfort in each of the following areas:

The ability to be attached and to attach.

The ability to be separate and set boundaries.

The ability to live with the good and bad of yourself and others.

The ability to establish yourself as an adult with appropriate adult authority.

Lay before God the areas where you have been hurt. Ask him to continue to bring those areas into the healing light of his grace. Let him know where you need him to give you courage to take steps into relationship so he can work some healing through his people. Thank him that, even as you pray this prayer, he is already at work developing these traits and making you more like him.

PART TWO

Helpful and Harmful Hiding

CHAPTER EIGHT

Helpful Hiding: Dealing with Suffering

❖

T here are times in which we are to hide from, or avoid, certain types of danger or pain (Proverbs 22:3). Yet many people (like Connie) feel that they should not only endure whatever is thrown their way, but even volunteer for more pain because they view that as "suffering for Christ." This is not a biblical view. Much suffering we experience is neither for God's glory nor for our good. Without some types of self-protection, we suffer in destructive ways. There are good and bad reasons to withdraw from pain.

A BIBLICAL VIEW OF SUFFERING (PAGE 122)

We experience two kinds of pain in our lifetime. The first is physical pain; the second is emotional and spiritual pain. Primarily, emotional pain comes from problems in our relatedness to God, self, or others.

- When someone we love leaves us, we feel a loss in our hearts. This is a "good pain" because it is a sign that the person mattered to us. When have you felt "good pain"? Give an example or two.

- "Bad pain" is often the result of ignoring "good pain." If, for instance, we ignore the anger we feel when someone is unloving to us, that anger gets internalized, and that is "bad pain." When, if ever, have you been aware of feeling "bad pain"? Be specific about the circumstances.

- Physical and emotional pain interact constantly. Think of a single parent with too many daily burdens who develops migraines, or of a construction worker with a debilitating back injury that leads to depression. When, if ever, have you experienced an interaction between physical pain and emotional pain? Which seemed to contribute to the other? Describe the situation.

Let's define *suffering* as *what we experience when a need or wish goes unmet,* and let's remember that suffering can be a friend or an enemy.

TYPES OF SUFFERING (PAGE 123)

What we do with the suffering we encounter has to do with the meaning of the pain we are in. Some suffering experiences we are to embrace joyfully, and some we are to resist with all our strength.

RESPONDING TO SUFFERING

LEVEL I.	JUST (Learning wisdom)	UNJUST
LEVEL II.	UNPREVENTABLE (Learning the value of love)	PREVENTABLE
LEVEL III.	FULL HEART (Joyful suffering)	NEED FOR JUSTICE LIMITS ON EVIL (Responsible withdrawal)

- ***Level I: Just and Unjust Suffering:*** Just suffering is our teacher. Painful consequences of our actions teach us to be accountable for what God has given us.

  — When, if ever, have you experienced somewhat painful consequences of your behavior? What lesson did you learn—or could you have learned?

Psychological symptoms like depression, eating disorders, addictions, and compulsive behaviors are generally the fruit of a combination of two types of sin: sin done *by* us and sin done *to* us.

  — What psychological symptom(s), if any, have you (like Diane [page 124 of the text]) had to deal with? Identify the sin done *to* you that you were coping with and the sin done *by* you that became part of that coping.

Unjust suffering brings on pain that we don't deserve to experience—which brings us to the second question: Is my suffering preventable?

- ***Level II: Preventable and Unpreventable Suffering:*** Unpreventable, unjust suffering is a product of the Fall. God is a good parent, but he allows the freedom of others to do evil because of the high value he places on love. He gives us freedom to choose love or evil because he knows that love without freedom is slavery, compliance, and performance.

  — What kind of unpreventable, unjust suffering, if any, has touched your life?

  — Handling unpreventable suffering usually entails denial or grieving or both. What has been your response to the unpreventable suffering you have experienced?

— We are certainly to be agents of justice on earth, but we also need to enter the "house of mourning" over the injustices we can't control. Our grief allows us to accept our creatureliness and look to God as the final Judge. What suffering, either personal or what you see in the world around you, has prompted you to mourn?

Preventable, unjust suffering raises the question of love versus justice, a problem that leads to the third question: Is our suffering a matter of love or justice?

- **Level III: Joyful Suffering and Helpful Hiding:** The first reason for avoiding pain involves love and justice: When our ability to love is greater than our need for justice, we joyfully suffer. When our need for justice exceeds our ability to love, we responsibly withdraw. This "responsible withdrawal" is helpful hiding.

— Review the three examples of common opportunities to suffer or not suffer listed on page 128 of the text. Add two or three of your own.

— The principle set forth in 1 Peter 2:19–21 is that *suffering is the price tag of love.* An innocent suffering for the guilty—Jesus dying on the cross for your sin and mine—doesn't fit our concept of fairness, but it does show the supremacy of God's love. When, if ever, have you or someone you know done what Margie did for Alan (pages 129–30 of the text) and chosen love over justice? Describe the situation.

When the heart is empty or injured and has nothing to give, we need justice—in the form of support away from suffering—to become reconnected to God and others. We need to be loved and filled with love, joy, and gratitude, the fruit of God's Spirit of grace, if we are to suffer joyfully. If we are allowing ourselves to suffer because of fear, obligation, or guilt, we can't respond out of love.

— When, if ever, have you or someone you know suffered because of fear, obligation, or guilt? Describe the suffering and the fear, obligation, or guilt that motivated the acceptance of suffering. What would have been a healthier response?

Helpful hiding is the opposite of forcing ourselves to suffer resentfully (page 131 of the text). It takes wisdom to know how much deprivation we can take in a relationship before real damage occurs. *The biblical solution is to withdraw in order to protect the soul.* This means knowing when our need for justice is greater than our ability to love.

— In this context, withdrawal is not selfishness, but responsible stewardship. Some suffering is not "for Jesus' sake." When have you found yourself (or seen someone you know) in a situation that was too difficult, too painful, too destructive, or too injurious and needed to set limits? Describe the situation and outline the limits that you set or that would have been good for you to set.

Limiting evil is another reason for refusing to suffer wrongdoing. To ignore a friend's continual irresponsibility or evil is to deny him the lesson of learning from the consequences of his actions (Proverbs 27:5).

— When, if ever, have you denied someone the lesson of learning from consequences—or perhaps where are you denying someone now? Put differently, what evil are you *not* limiting?

— The more loved we are, the more we are able to withstand suffering from a loved position. Are you more like Lee or Raymond (pages 132–33 of the text) in background? in your current support system? and therefore in your ability to withstand suffering?

If you can recognize and accept that both love and justice exist, and that God has provided some clear provisions for dealing with these coexisting realities, perhaps you will come to a decision to endure suffering in a Christ-like way. Seeking out loving relationships will do a lot to help you prepare for suffering when it comes. Withdrawing from injustice when you recognize it will protect you from unnecessary suffering.

PRINCIPLES VERSUS RULES (PAGE 134)

The "love versus justice" principle may be frustrating for some Christians who would like more defined "rules of conduct" about suffering. They may feel a little lost without specific guidelines for the particular kinds of situations in which they should or shouldn't allow themselves to suffer.

• Explain in your own words why following principles is more demanding than following rules.

• When, if ever, have you seen allegiance to rules take precedence over acting in love?

Jesus' summation of the entire Law in loving God and people (Matthew 22:37–40) was a slap in the face of religious tradition. Tradition had taken the place of a relationship with God.

HELPFUL HIDING (PAGE 134)

Sometimes we need to withdraw from dangerous or hurtful situations.

- What are your criteria for knowing when to withdraw?

Hurtful situations can arise from two sources: internal pain (including our thoughts, feelings, and memories) and external pain (occurring primarily in our present relationships). To learn how to deal with both sources of pain, let's continue to look at helpful hiding.

REMEMBER JENNY

Jenny endured an incredible amount of deep suffering in a short period of time. Within a few hours she went from loving, warm attachment to terror and complete alienation. Yet she survived because she had a history of consistent bonding with her parents. They had given her an excellent picture of love and faithfulness in relationship.

- Who, if anyone, has offered you a clear picture of love and faithfulness in relationship? If you haven't yet been blessed with such a picture, where might you go to find one?

- Who, if anyone, could you help give a clear picture of love and faithfulness in relationship? Ask God to help you handle that privilege and responsibility with wisdom.

Coming Out of Hiding

1. Suffering (defined as what we experience when a need or wish goes unmet) that is neither for God's glory or our good is one good reason for hiding. Give at least one example from your own life of just suffering (the kind we are to experience joyfully) and unjust suffering (from which we should responsibly withdraw). How would you respond to the objection, "Avoiding pain is an expression of selfishness"? What current injustice would you be wise to withdraw from in order to protect yourself from unnecessary suffering? What current injustice would you be wise to withdraw from in order to limit evil?

2. We can endure more suffering and deprivation in the present if we have had enough consistent, warm, accepting attachment in the past. What does this fact help you understand about how well you have or haven't coped with tough times in the past? What loving relationships are you experiencing that will help you bear up when suffering comes again? What will you do to begin experiencing such relationships if you currently find yourself feeling isolated and alone?

3. Ask God to give you insight about your life and to show you where you should be withdrawing from injustice; where you should be withdrawing in order to limit evil; and where you can find loving relationships that will help prepare you for future suffering.

CHAPTER NINE

Helpful Hiding: Preparing for Relationship

✛

D wight's twenty minutes of puttering in the garage after work every day illustrates the purpose of helpful hiding: It is not to isolate, but to withdraw. To isolate is to remove oneself from relationship; it has a permanent component. *Withdrawal is a temporary distancing so that the heart can regroup itself to reattach.*

- When we withdraw, we remove ourselves from the pain or injury or distractions that keep us from love. When, if ever, has someone's withdrawal caused you to misunderstand that person? And when, if ever, has your withdrawal caused someone to misunderstand you?

- To reenter relationship doesn't always mean we reattach with the person who hurt us. Some relationships need permanent limits put on them because the person doesn't have God's values. Give an example or two.

Quite often people in a relationship need time apart, especially if there has been injury on either side from elements such as hostility, chronic irresponsibility, hypercriticism, or betrayal of trust. To attempt closeness too soon is to risk reinjuring an already damaged heart. That is why we are to be discerning and careful before moving into vulnerability in relationships too quickly.

HELPFUL HIDING REQUIRES RESPONSIBILITY (PAGE 139)

Helpful hiding—responsible withdrawal—involves deliberation, prayerful awareness, and conscious choice. It is a component of wisdom. It is not reactive, automatic, or impulsive. Helpful hiding isn't a knee-jerk response. And helpful hiding is always truthful.

• What do you appreciate about Michelle's example of helpful hiding?

• What past (or present) situation in your life—or in the life of someone you know—might have merited helpful hiding? Modeling your response after Michelle's approach, answer these three questions: What would you have told the person(s) involved? What honest reason(s) for withdrawing would you have given? How would you have wanted to cope with the person's response?

BARRIERS TO HELPFUL HIDING (PAGE 139)

It is not the easiest thing in the world to protect ourselves from pain. Though it is our responsibility as stewards of our souls, several forces are at work to undermine our attempts to withdraw responsibly.

• Four forces are defined on page 140 of the text. Below, note which ones interfere with your ability or even your desire to withdraw responsibly.

— Fear of isolation

— Fear of injury or attack

— Naïveté

— Repetition compulsion

- What do the descriptions of these barriers suggest to you about the source of these barriers in your life?

- What do the descriptions of these barriers suggest about their remedy?

TYPES OF HELPFUL HIDING (PAGE 141)

God has provided many ways to deal with spiritual, emotional, and relational pain. These methods of helpful hiding can help us stay in relationship, not in denial. Our helpful patterns keep us from injury, debilitating pain, or mistreatment by others. Yet they bow to love. These hiding patterns never keep the soul out of connection. They allow us to stay in contact with God and caring people.

- **Emotional Helpful Hiding:** We all have a storehouse of painful memories, feelings, and thoughts inside. If we were to feel the impact of all of these emotions simultaneously, we would run the risk of losing touch with reality. Our ability to experience emotional pain is measured by the amount and quality of love we have received over the years.

— Which of the following examples of emotional hiding (defined on pages 142–43 of the text) have helped you, or could have helped you, in the past?

Anticipation

Forgiveness

Perspective

Humor

Patience

Adjusting (compensation)

Confession

Making restitution

Putting it on hold (mature sublimation)

— Which of the nine options just listed offer you a good method for dealing with a current situation? Describe what you will do.

- ***Relational Helpful Hiding:*** Not only do we experience painful memories and feelings inside, but we also encounter destructive situations outside: that is, in our present relationships. Much of the work we need to do here involves learning to set appropriate limits on the irresponsibility or selfishness of others.

  — Setting a verbal boundary is a clear way to take ownership of your soul. The word *no* is a good example. When have (or when could have) verbal limits helped you deal responsibly with evil done against you? Be specific.

  — At times our *no* is not heard or respected. The limits we need then are more geographical in nature, such as leaving the room, leaving the house, or calling for help. When have (or when could have) physical limits helped you deal responsibly with evil done against you? Be specific.

  — Review Jesus' four-level program for limiting evil against us in Matthew 18:15–17. When, if ever, have you seen the wisdom of first going in private to a person who has hurt you? When has involving two or three witnesses been necessary and helpful—or when would it have been? What kinds of situations would call for an intervention with the church? with expulsion?

  — What current situation calls for you to set verbal or physical limits? What will you do—and when will you take that step?

JENNY'S SUFFERING (PAGE 144)

God never intended that we embrace all forms of suffering. Like Jenny, we must learn when to accept pain and when to resist evil. Hiding can be the most caring and responsible thing to do in many situations, as long as its ultimate aim is for us to reenter a loving relationship.

- Jenny did the responsible thing when she hid in the old oak tree—and then she thanked the oak for being in the path and marking her escape route. Think through the appropriate hiding skills you have learned and how certain relationships, primarily with God and with significant other people in your life, have contributed to your relational skills. Then, like Jenny did to the oak tree, thank God for placing those ancient oaks in your path that he designed as markers for escaping evil.

- In addition, you may want to thank certain friends and family members for their parts in helping you shape certain skills—even at times when it was painful.

Jenny might never have seen her parents again had she not learned how to hide responsibly from the evil that confronted her in the enemy soldiers. We also face such obstacles, yet in the long run they can prove to be instruments that help us learn appropriate hiding skills. In the next chapter let's look at harmful ways of hiding that God never intended for us.

Coming Out of Hiding

1. Helpful hiding is about withdrawal, not isolation. Withdrawal is a temporary distancing so that the heart can regroup itself to reattach. Do you, like Dwight and like Jesus himself (Matthew 14:23), function better when you get regular, if not daily, alone time? Describe what that time does for you. What do—or will—you do to get the kind of alone time you need?

2. Helpful hiding patterns are like sentries that protect our soul from injury, debilitating pain, or mistreatment by others, yet they never keep us out of relationships. Review the lists of helpful hiding patterns on pages 142–44 of the text. Which patterns have served you well? Give specific examples from your life. Should you put into practice one of these types of helpful hiding today? When will you take the first step?

3. Thank God for the different patterns of helpful hiding and the protection he gives through them. Ask God to help you learn when to accept pain and when to resist evil and to teach you to recognize when hiding can be the most caring and responsible thing to do.

CHAPTER TEN

Harmful Hiding: Six Critical Stages
✥

Remember Doug and his mother? He didn't feel the sadness of loss, because there was no relationship to mourn. The extent to which we attach deeply to God and others is the extent to which we leave something behind in people's hearts. If we allow ourselves to matter to others, and them to us, we will miss them and they will miss us.

Hiding moves in two directions. It helps when it means withdrawing from injury of some sort, but it harms when it means avoiding the good things God has for us.

WHAT IS HARMFUL HIDING? (PAGE 148)

Helpful hiding is appropriate self-protection. Its design is to help us withdraw responsibly and prepare for loving reattachment. *Harmful hiding* is also self-protection, but it *protects us from the very grace and truth we need.* The one distinctive that always points to harmful hiding is its fruit: *isolation.* The more we hide, the more grace we need.

- People generally don't go through life as self-protectively as Doug's mother without having experienced some serious emotional injury or deprivation. Most likely, some destructive relationships had taught her that it is not safe to be open and vulnerable. When have you (or someone you know) hidden from relationships and isolated yourself from the grace that heals? What injury was behind that harmful hiding?

- The only way Doug's mother could have been restored would have been to begin allowing herself to be slowly and gently connected to safe relationships. And relationships were the thing of which she was most frightened. When, if ever, have you lived (or seen someone else live) this dilemma?

A DEVELOPMENTAL VIEW OF THE SELF (PAGE 149)

Where do harmful hiding patterns come from? We need to look at early child development to answer that question.

- In preparation for later exploring how these three developmental processes can be used defensively, briefly define each. Also note the adult abilities for which they help prepare you.

  1. Introjection

  2. Projection

  3. Splitting

Before seeing how these three developmental processes can be used in defensive ways, let's look at the series of events that lead to the development of harmful hiding patterns.

HOW WE FORM HARMFUL HIDING PATTERNS (PAGE 150)

We do not invent destructive hiding styles out of thin air. Harmful hiding begins instead with our needs. That is the first stage.

- **Stage One: Our Needs Go Unmet:** Our four basic emotional and spiritual developmental needs (attachment, separateness, resolving our good and bad selves, and authority and adulthood [addressed in chapters 4–7]) are the starting point for understanding how we develop harmful hiding patterns.

  — Parents are sinners who have also been sinned against. They aren't going to meet their children's needs correctly at all times. Which of the four areas do you need to shore up for your own good as well as for any parenting you do, or may someday do?

- **Stage Two: We Experience Injury to Our Soul:** Nowhere is the evidence of the Fall more apparent than in the universal experience of emotional injury in childhood. Things go wrong in everyone's childhood.

  — Which of the four primary reasons why things go wrong in childhood (listed here) did you experience? Which of the four are your own children experiencing?

  A lack of love in the parents (their own sinfulness)

  A lack of ability in the parents (the sins of their parents)

The child's contributions (his or her own sinfulness)

Circumstantial consequences of the Fall (accidental trauma, death of a parent, socioeconomic factors, physical limitations, and so on)

— When a legitimate, God-given need goes unmet because of neglect or attack, that part of us goes into shock. Such injury doesn't necessarily lead to harmful hiding patterns. When has a childhood injury (to you or to someone you know) not resulted in patterns of harmful hiding?

Injuries heal much more quickly when we keep short accounts, take mutual responsibility, and express love. Then the injured part of the soul is quickly brought back into relationship and not left in isolation. The longer and deeper the isolation, the greater the injury—and the greater the chances for hurtful hiding patterns. The longer that part of the self is in isolation, the more it becomes a "bad" part. We lose the growth process when we are removed from grace and truth.

— When, if ever, have you experienced the healing that comes from keeping short accounts, taking mutual responsibility, and expressing love? Describe what happened in both the situation and the relationship.

— Parents who can deal with the logs in their own eyes and who can then admit errors to their children will minimize the effects of their parenting errors. Then there is no confusion inside the child's heart about why they hurt. The child of the confessing parent doesn't have to bear the burden of the errors all by herself. What does this truth say to you if you are a parent? What logs in your own eyes do you need to deal with? If you are not sure, ask the Lord and ask your spouse.

We need to remember that not only do others injure us, but we also injure ourselves by our own sinful nature. We need to confess our sins to friends who will love and support us rather than condemn us so that those sins don't lead us to harmful hiding.

• **Stage Three: We Make Legitimate Needs Bad:** When a pervasive, sinful, and unrepentant pattern of relating in the family persists, it affects the child in a very negative way. When there are chronic dysfunctional patterns of relating, a different mechanism takes over: *The legitimate emotional need is made bad.*

— Children blame the need rather than the parents who didn't meet that need, because children can't tolerate the idea that parents could be failing them. A child's perceived omnipotence (one of the Fall's consequences is that children believe they are the center of the world) also leads them to blame the need. Perceived omnipotence can also cause the child to take responsibility for her injuries. What insight about yourself, if any, does this discussion offer you? What legitimate emotional needs have you made bad and what contributed to that?

— Jesus validated our neediness (Luke 4:18). When we express our needs, we move toward connecting with him and others. Give an example or two of this from your own life (ideally) or someone else's.

Injury to our needs and isolation of those needs, caused by denial, lack of confession, or lack of forgiveness, plow fertile ground for the next step in developing harmful hiding patterns.

• **Stage Four: *We Deny Our Own Needs:*** When our heart is injured and isolated, it doesn't stop with blaming our needs. It moves beyond that to a *denial* of our needs. Our injured soul demands that we forget this "troublesome" part of us ever existed.

— Denial is behaving, thinking, or feeling as if some reality about us is not true. What reality about yourself have you denied or are you in denial about today? Be as specific as possible.

Reality perception is primarily relational. We learn reality mainly from our attachments, especially in the impressionable and formative years of childhood. We learn to affirm those parts of ourselves that keep us in relationship and to deny the existence of those parts that isolate us. If our significant relationships have God's values and perceptions at heart, we are that much closer to reality. But if we who are closest to their heart have unbiblical values in some places, our children will accept those distorted values as true.

— Look at yourself and your childhood through this lens. What parts of yourself kept you in relationship with your parents? What parts isolated you from them? Due to that isolation, what parts of you do you deny or have you denied in the past? Consider, for instance, your need and longing for closeness, your separateness and freedom, your badness, your adult parts.

— It is common for people who have been injured and isolated to grow up prematurely, becoming "small adults" at a very early age. In what ways, if any, were you a "small adult"? Be specific.

— Denial can extend to not only your needs, but even to the actual memories surrounding those needs. Beyond that, people who have had to develop a "false self" often have memory denial. Where, if at all, do you see yourself in these statements? What memories have you repressed? What kind of performing does your false self do?

Denial of our need puts us on the road to developing harmful hiding patterns. It is the lie that gives rise to false answers for meeting our real needs.

- **Stage Five: We Develop False Solutions:** When we deny the existence of our spiritual and emotional needs, we develop coping patterns that help us adapt to the loss of a part of our soul. These patterns protect us from further injury and help us survive, but what emerges are actually harmful hiding patterns. We will look at specific hiding patterns in the next chapter. For now, it is important to realize that the defenses we develop as children emerge for a good reason. We experience genuine danger: the threat of losing relationship at some level. If it weren't for that danger, that potential loss of relationship, we would have no need for the hiding pattern.

  — The problem with these defenses, this denial, is that we can't fix what we deny. In other words, denial leads to the inability to take responsibility for some aspect of our lives. Also, denial usually leads to fear of others. When have you seen this inability to take responsibility and/or this fear of other people either in someone you know or in yourself? Describe the evidence.

  — The kinds of people we shy away from can be a clue to what our unloved, undeveloped, and denied needs could be. Take some time to consider what kinds of people you shy away from. What clues, if any, does that pattern give you about the injured parts of your own soul?

Again, the kinds of people we shy away from can be a clue to what our unloved, undeveloped, and denied needs could be. We are hiding destructively when we hate what we need.

- **Stage Six: We Produce Bad Fruit:** Ultimately, when our needs aren't met, we will experience some problem in living. This is generally experienced in the form of symptoms like depression, anxiety, panic attacks, addictive and compulsive behaviors, marital tensions, job difficulties, and physiological disorders.

  — When, if ever, have you realized that you had been denying your needs? What symptom(s) did you experience?

Symptoms always occur because of the law of sowing and reaping God has built into the universe. Evil done to us by others or by ourselves has a consequence.

  — Many Christians are confused about their symptoms, thinking that relational, emotional, or task-related struggles are the real problem. This confusion is generally the result of a lack of safe relationships. What "grace and truth" relationship(s) were you connected to when your symptoms of denial appeared? What "grace and truth" relationship(s) are you currently connected to as you work through this *Hiding from Love* study?

Darkness always needs the light of unconditional love to give up its secrets. Once people become connected to a "grace and truth" relationship, their symptoms begin making more sense to them.

SUMMARY (PAGE 163)

The six stages of developing hiding patterns are not a one-time event. Though they generally begin in the early years, they continue throughout life.

- What evidence in your own life, if any, have you seen that these stages of developing hiding patterns weren't unique to your early years? Be specific.

Defenses have a cyclical nature; what is denied tends to be more split off as time goes by, and what is broken gets more broken over time.

• Where have you seen evidence of this truth in your life or the life of someone you know?

How do we recognize our harmful hiding patterns? How can we tell when we are being wisely careful and when we are being resistant to love?

REMEMBER JENNY

Jenny's isolation caused her to see her needs as demanding, selfish, and destructive. What God had created good, Jenny's disconnected heart began to call bad.

• Are you, like Jenny, in a disconnected state? Do you isolate yourself from God and the very relationships that he has put in your path to help you? Are you hiding from love?

• As a result of your aloneness, what legitimate spiritual and emotional needs have you called bad? What legitimate spiritual and emotional needs have others called bad? Have you been denying what has had a "bad" label? Have you denied your own legitimate emotional needs?

Learn the six critical stages of harmful hiding, and reflect carefully on your own condition. Rest in God's grace as you evaluate your life to find the harmful ways you may be hiding from legitimate needs and loving relationships.

Coming Out of Hiding

1. Hiding helps when it means withdrawing from injury and preparing for loving reattachment, but it harms when it means avoiding the good things—the grace and truth we need and which God has for us. Harmful hiding develops in stages. Review the discussion of Stage Two (pages 151–55 of the text) and Angela's story. Which of your developmental needs (chapters 4–7) went unmet? What injuries to your soul resulted? What legitimate emotional need(s) did you make bad? What needs did you learn to deny?

2. When we fail to address our needs adequately, we produce "bad fruit" or symptoms. What bad fruit can result from denying the need to be attached (close, bonded) to others? from denying the need to be separate (say no, set limits)? from denying the need to be forgiven for being partly good and partly bad rather than being either all good or unforgivably bad? from denying the need to take adult authority? (Some examples of bad fruit are listed on page 161 of the text.)

3. Prayerfully consider whether any bad fruit in your life might be evidence of harmful hiding. Lay before God the symptoms you see in yourself. Ask him to open your eyes to legitimate emotional needs you are denying and to ways you may be hiding from love. Finally, ask him to deal with the root of that bad fruit and bring healing to your soul. One way he will do that is to move you away from isolation and into relationship with himself and with his people. So also ask him to give you the courage to take that step.

CHAPTER ELEVEN

Harmful Hiding: The Results

✦

As Marshall and Judy's dialogue points out, it is difficult to know when our self-protective behaviors, thoughts, or feelings are helpful or harmful. Judy thought Marshall's hiding was harmful, while Marshall saw it as healthy and normal. So, switching from the past and the origins of harmful hiding to the present, let's look at the most important characteristics of destructive self-protection. We will be answering the question, *How can we understand our own patterns of relating?*

ISOLATION (PAGE 166)

The most telling aspect of our harmful hiding patterns is that they never stop with simply protecting us from evil or danger: *they isolate us from what we need to grow.* And one result of isolation is losing grace (unconditional relationship) and truth (reality that we need). These two dynamics are the main ingredients of spiritual and emotional growth.

- When have you seen or, ideally, experienced the growth that can result from grace and truth? Who offered you a relationship of unconditional love and acceptance? What aspects of truth did that person hold out?

Remember Ron? His withdrawing of his attachment needs was obvious. But when we hide our needs for separateness, honesty, and boundaries in relationships, it is a different situation. Mary had hidden from her separateness. Her caring was easy to see, but her honesty wasn't. She avoided confrontations by always compromising and keeping the peace.

- What needs might you be hiding in relationships—your need for grace? separateness? honesty? boundaries?

Another result of the harmful hiding pattern of isolation is that we resent or fear what we need. Harmful hiding can make us, like Wayne, hate what we really need the most.

- What good things that relationships offer do you fear—intimacy? vulnerability? risk? dependency? accountability? Step back from that fear and remind yourself why you need those very things.

LOSS OF FREEDOM AND RESPONSIBILITY (PAGE 169)

While helpful hiding patterns are generally the well-thought-out products of choices, harmful hiding patterns are reactive, automatic, and often unconscious. The result is that we lose our precious freedom.

- Faye had lost the freedom to be open about what was going on inside her. She had developed the strong defense of immediately switching subjects when a "bad" part of her came into relationship. What freedom have you lost due to any harmful hiding you may do? Or what freedom has someone you know lost because of his or her harmful patterns of hiding?

God places a high premium on our being able to autonomously choose to protect ourselves rather than to react angrily or violently (Proverbs 3:31).

Choice is a product of being attached to God and others and of being responsible for what God has entrusted to you. Reactivity is a product of fear. It only furthers our isolation.

- Think about your interactions with people. What patterns of reacting (if any) are you aware of? What are the triggers, and what is your reaction?

- What is the connection between responsibility and choice? Why doesn't reactivity lead to responsibility?

- Why is choice a frightening proposition to some people? Why does being attached to God and to people help us make choices? (How well connected to God and to people are you?)

In addition to isolation, a second major result of harmful hiding is denial. Let's look at the results of this kind of defense.

DENIAL (PAGE 171)

In our early years, our needs for attachment, separateness, forgiveness, and authority can be perceived as bad. That perception can become denial that these needs even exist, which is our way of protecting them from being reinjured. But when one or more of these four basic needs is damaged, split off, and hidden, the ripple effect shows at some level in our lives.

- How can you tell if denial is your method of harmful hiding? One important indicator is shame. Shame is a sense of "badness" about ourselves that urges us to withdraw further from relationship. It tells us the lie that something about us is beyond grace and beyond relationship. On a scale of 1 to 10, to what degree is shame an issue in your life? Let 1 be "Shame? Why would I feel shame?" and 10 be "It's a black hole about to swallow me up!"

- Shame is a tool Satan uses to keep us from reestablishing relationship to God and one another. Why would Satan want to do that? And when, if ever, have you experienced him at work in your life in this way? Specifically, when has shame kept you from establishing or reestablishing your relationship with God? your relationships with other people?

Shame is a prime motivator for harmful hiding. When we are ashamed of our needs, we can't feel safe about bringing them to the cross or anywhere else.

- What needs, if any, are you ashamed of? Or what part(s) of yourself are you most ashamed of—your neediness? your appearance? a sexual or substance abuse problem? something in your past?

- Shame is telling you to hide. The only biblical response to shame is to disobey it. God commands, "Confess the badness to God and others" (see James 5:16; 1 John 1:9). Confess the badness to God right now. Afterwards, to what safe person will you confess your badness?

Confession brings up the difference between humiliation and humility. Humiliation is the result of experiencing our badness outside of relationship. Humility, on the other hand, is experiencing our badness within the confines of love. Humility brings us back to our need for God and his resources.

- We always have a responsibility to humble ourselves—that is, to bring our needs to God and his people. It is the first step toward sanctification. What brokenness do you need to confess to God and others? Do so now.

Humility leads to confession of our sin and brokenness to God and others; humility helps us live and grow effectively in an evil, fallen world. But humiliation is the evidence of shameful hiding.

LIVING IN THE PAST (PAGE 174)

Pam grew up in a family that emphasized connection while ignoring the legitimate need for boundaries. So, in her twenties, Pam was experiencing a "cold heart" resulting from a hidden separation conflict. Her problem illustrates another aspect of harmful hiding: the past becomes the present.

- When we are injured in some area of the heart, that part isolates itself for a period of time. Since the injured parts of ourselves remain fixed and unfinished, they can function no better than their maturity level. What part of yourself seems unfinished? Explain why you answered as you did.

- We can't "do" something with what we don't have. In fact, to demand that people be more mature than they are is to place them under condemnation. Adults whose independent parts have been frozen in the past need to move these aspects of character into grace and truth. They will have to take risks, learn about consequences, and then practice, practice, practice. If you have been able to identify an unfinished part of you, at what point are you in this process of helping that part catch up?

Instead of going into denial about our past, we are to heal the parts of our soul that are still locked in the past in their injured state. In a very real sense, as long as those injured parts remain unhealed, we are living in the past.

- Another term for this confusion of past and present is *transference.* Transference occurs when our feelings toward someone in the past affect our present relationships. When, if ever, have you been aware of this confusion in your own life? Be specific about the person in the past and the present situation. ("You're like my mother/father" is a typical example.)

- Transference signals that an injury is making itself known. It indicates that sad, angry, hurt, frightened, or loving feelings from the past are struggling to be brought out of isolation. Look again at the situation you just identified. What feelings from the past were wanting to come out of isolation?

- Transference tells us that an injured part of our soul is still disconnected and therefore in hiding. In which of the following examples (if any) do you see yourself?

  — The person with attachment injuries may see others as too needy, intrusive, or demanding.

  — The person with separation injuries may see others as controlling or irresponsible.

— The person with good/bad injuries may see others either as idealized or as constantly letting him or her down.

— The person with authority injuries may see others as critical and parental.

- What will you do with whatever you just realized about yourself?

It is important to examine and learn from consistent patterns of relating styles we find ourselves in. The more we can separate out transference (seeing life through the filter of our past reality) from sound judgment (seeing life in its present reality), the better our relationships become.

JENNY'S TRANSFERENCE AND OURS (PAGE 181)

The second time Jenny spied the soldiers in the woods, she immediately transferred her feelings about the past. With greater speed and skill this time, she again eluded them. She never took the time to consider that the men in uniform might not be the enemy.

- Jenny's act was harmful to her even though she had no idea that she was acting against her own interests. When, if ever, have you been aware that a past pattern of helpful hiding (yours or someone else's) had become harmful? Be specific about why that hiding pattern was no longer needed.

- Do you find the past in any way infiltrating the present, protecting—or harming—your present relationships? Again, be specific.

Once we understand our own patterns of relating through the signals that tell us we are in harmful hiding patterns, we are on the road to positive change. But before we focus on moving out of harmful hiding patterns, it is important to understand the cost of harmful hiding, the subject of the next chapter.

Coming Out of Hiding

1. Harmful hiding isolates us from what we need to grow: We lose grace (unconditional, loving relationships) and truth (information we need), and we resent, fear, or even hate what we need most. A second major result of harmful hiding is denial that our needs exist, and shame is an indicator that denial is our method of harmful hiding. Shame is a sense of badness that urges us to withdraw further from relationship. Another aspect of harmful hiding is that the past exerts so much control over the present that the past becomes the present. Our feelings toward someone in the past affect our present relationships. Which aspect of harmful hiding have you dealt with most: isolation, denial and shame, or transference? What will you do this week to move out of isolation? What will you do to disobey shame's command to conceal the "badness"? (To whom will you confess your badness?) Or what will you do to try to figure out what the transference is telling you about your injured parts?

2. With all the negative consequences of harmful hiding, why do you suppose we tend to do it anyway?

3. Talk with God about your patterns of harmful hiding and what you have experienced as you have tried to get free of those hiding styles. Share your fears and frustrations, thank him for your victories, and ask him to continue to bring healing and freedom to your life.

CHAPTER TWELVE
The Cost of Harmful Hiding
❖

E dward had developed a harmful hiding pattern of distracting verbalization. Its function was to protect him from deep or uncomfortable intimacy. Talking became Edward's way of controlling closeness at a manageable level. His drug problem, however, signaled that his verbalization wasn't doing a perfect job.

- Someone in Eric's group noticed that he was a "nervous talker," that he would start conversations or ask questions for no apparent reason. Often we have a clearer perspective on other people's hiding patterns than on our own. When, if ever, have you noticed a behavioral pattern in someone's life that suggests he or she is hiding from love?

- Who, if anyone, might you ask about behavioral patterns in your life that might indicate that you are hiding from love?

When we hide, the time and energy that we need to spend in loving and being loved is diverted; it is channeled instead into maintaining our isolation.

- Being human means having built-in limits. We have only a certain amount of energy and resources available to us to use within our limited life span. On what few important tasks does God want us to focus? See Micah 6:8.

- What does Jesus' teaching in Matthew 13:12 say to you about the value of taking the risk and bringing the hidden parts of yourself into the light?

When we own or "have" ourselves, Jesus says, our heart is enlarged. But when we keep part of ourselves in darkness, we deny its existence. We "don't have," and our heart is less accessible to growth. The cost of harmful hiding, then, is a lack of love and an increase of bad fruit.

THE COST IN REINJURY (PAGE 185)

We have seen that harmful hiding doesn't work. Destructive defenses don't really protect us from being hurt again. In fact, they contribute to the worsening of our developmental deficits. When we hide in harmful ways that isolate us, we imprison the injured part of ourselves with our destructive memories. Those who injured us in the past become the only relationships available to our hurt self. Thus, in hiding, we constantly relive our hurts.

- Remember Angela from chapter 10? Whenever she tried to say no to someone, her mother's face would show up, sad and hurt, with trembling lips and a single tear trickling down her face. What images, words, or memories from your past help keep you in hiding?

- Angela's undeveloped need for separateness would have benefited greatly from her being with people who celebrated and relished her boundaries. Who in your life could celebrate the undeveloped need(s) you have identified? Or where can you go to find safe relationships?

- In Luke 11:24–27, Jesus points out that a spiritually empty heart—that is, one caught in isolation—is susceptible to being plunged back into the injuries of the past. It is important to note that the heart of the person in the passage is "swept and put in order." The person has not moved toward God, but has tried to deal with his heart in isolation from God! In what ways, if any, are you trying to deal with your wounded heart in isolation from God? Or are you letting your emptiness and pain move you toward God and his people? Explain the reason why you chose either isolation or connection.

As isolation deepens, memories recur and reinjure the child countless times over the years. Only when there is an intervention of safe attachment into that hurt, trusting part of the soul can there be relief from the repetition of the damage.

THE COST OF STAYING IN HIDING (PAGE 187)

Remember Jenny. Her experience illustrates how easy it is to stay in hiding once it becomes a familiar place. Just as Jenny could no longer distinguish her countrymen from invaders, our hiding patterns prevent us from being open to the people, truths, and experiences that God makes available to help us mature spiritually.

- What was Jenny missing out on when she thought the second group of soldiers were enemies?

- What are you missing out on by staying in your familiar hiding places?

The final aspect of harmful hiding is that our choices of hiding styles are related to what we are protecting in ourselves. In other words, our defensive patterns are specific to our injuries. Learning to discern your own specific tendencies in hiding can give you important insight into your growth needs. Our specific hiding patterns are the subject of the chapters in the last part of this book.

Coming Out of Hiding

1. Harmful hiding doesn't really protect us from being hurt again. Instead, as Angela's story illustrates, we imprison the injured part of ourselves with our destructive memories. What destructive memories imprison you? How have these memories caused you to repeatedly relive your hurts?

2. Our choices of hiding are related to what we are protecting in ourselves: our defensive patterns are specific to our injuries. When have you seen this truth in your life or the life of someone you know? Explain how the defensive pattern was a logical result of the injury sustained earlier.

3. Ask God to help you own, or take responsibility for, your life, specifically for the parts of yourself you have hidden. Also ask God to help you stop your efforts to clean up your heart on your own (Luke 11:24–27). Ask him for the courage and hope you need to let your pain move you toward him and his people.

PART THREE

Hope for Those in Hiding

How can you know which need or injury you are dealing with? Your hiding style gives you some clues, but as you may have noticed, some hiding styles fit more than one issue.

For example, some people become perfectionists in order to cope with their internal isolation and lack of relationship inside. Their perfectionism keeps them away from their sense of aloneness. Others become perfectionists in order to cope with an inability to feel loved when they fail. People in the first category will tend to have an inability to need and depend on people; they will struggle with trusting others. People in the second category may be more unable to deal well with failure, grief, and receiving forgiveness.

To discover the issues you need to address, you probably need to go beyond looking only at patterns of behavior that suggest your hiding style. In addition, consider factors such as what types of relational conflicts you encounter, troublesome emotions and experiences with which you struggle, and feedback from others.

Chapter Thirteen

Hiding from Attachment

✣

This chapter and the next three discuss our hiding mechanisms in depth. Not every aspect of these chapters will necessarily relate to your specific need. I recommend that you read all four chapters, because we all struggle at some level with all of these issues. If you are in a rush, however, just turn to the chapter that addresses the hiding mechanisms related to that part of your soul you are convinced is injured most deeply.

We all hide in harmful ways, many unknown to us. But we need more than the knowledge that hiding is part of our lives and relationships. We also need to know what our specific hiding patterns, or styles, are. And just as important, we need to understand what our patterns mean for us.

- Hiding styles are a "road map" to our developmental needs. Our protective patterns help point out to us what it is they are keeping safe (a broken trusting part, an injured will, a hurt imperfect self, or a bruised authority need). Think back on some of the people you have met in this study. Choose two people from among Stuart (chapter 4), Cathy (chapter 5), Carol (chapter 6), or Phil (chapter 7) and show how that person's hiding style points to his or her developmental needs.

- Understanding our hiding styles also helps us make sense of the loss of freedom that comes along with them. Because they are reactive, defenses don't always allow us time to deliberate over a prudent course of action. This loss of freedom often causes conflicts in relationships and feelings of regret later. What reactive patterns do you notice in your own life? What could those patterns be hiding? Again, consider a broken trusting part, an injured will, a hurt imperfect self, or a bruised authority need.

KEYS TO UNDERSTANDING OUR STYLES (PAGE 194)

Before we actually look at our particular hiding styles, we should examine four general truths about them. These truths are good reminders of how pervasive these strategies are in all our lives.

- Review the discussion on pages 194–96 of the text. What about any or all of the following truths was especially interesting, surprising, or helpful?

— We all use a variety of styles.

— Some hiding styles overlap: we employ some "all-purpose" patterns for more than one developmental need. So, as I mentioned above, beyond looking at patterns of behavior that suggest your hiding style, also consider your emotional and behavioral symptoms, types of relational conflicts you have, patterns in your behavior and your relationships, and information about yourself from people who know you well.

— Our hiding styles are always opposite to the protected part of the soul, and the reaction of darkness to light (wanting to stay out of the light and urging us to stay hidden) is also operating in our defensive styles.

— All harmful hiding styles have denial of some sort of reality about our souls at their core. The essence of any defense is that it causes us to act, feel, or think a lie. This lie is basically that a legitimate, God-ordained part of ourselves doesn't exist.

We will be exploring our hiding styles according to the developmental need with which they occur. We will also look at the fundamental fear that surrounds each injury. First, note that our harmful hiding patterns fall into two groups: internal hiding and relational hiding styles.

TWO GROUPS OF HIDING STYLES (PAGE 196)

Internal hiding styles are those patterns we use to hide from our painful internal feelings, thoughts, or memories. Our *relational hiding styles* are those patterns of dealing with the world that protect us from the perceived danger of the world. If the injury being protected is deep enough and damaging enough, the defensive style will be so much a part of the person's everyday life that it seems like a part of the soul.

- Which style seems more prevalent in your life? Are you more often hiding from yourself or hiding from others? Support your answer with specifics. If you are not sure, keep reading. We will be looking at examples of each.

- What hope does the gospel message offer us whose styles are deeply entrenched in our hearts? See, for instance, John 8:36.

INTERNAL HIDING FROM ATTACHMENT (PAGE 198)

When our need for attachment, or our "*yes* muscle," is injured, we tend to view relationship itself as the danger. Our ability to trust God and others may have been violated by abandonment, abuse, detachment, superficial family intimacy, and other injuries.

- The fear that our needy parts will cause our emotional annihilation gives rise to internal hiding. When, if ever, have you feared that your own needs and dependencies would engulf or overwhelm you? When, if ever, have you feared that others would betray or hurt you because of your needs? What behavior resulted from that fear?

The overwhelming terror we experience when our unmet needs for connection and our needy parts come face to face causes tremendously powerful hiding patterns. We will look at six styles of internal hiding from attachment.

- ***The "Log and Speck" Style (Projection):*** When we expel our bad parts onto others, we see them as having the log that is actually blinding us. We are to learn to humbly take responsibility for our own log before correcting someone else's speck.

  — What was Leigh projecting onto the poor and homeless she saw in her city? What did that reveal about her?

  — What, if anything, are you projecting on someone? Be specific about both the what and the who.

- ***Emotional Picture Style (Introjection):*** In this hiding pattern, we place traits of other significant people onto ourselves. Good emotional pictures eventually help us be "rooted and grounded in love." But, just as we become more like the loving people we allow inside, the opposite can happen also.

— What had Barry introjected? What neediness did this introjection reveal?

— Of what negative introjecting, if any, are you aware? What have been some of the consequences of this introjection?

- **_Black and White Style (Splitting):_** For individuals with attachment injuries, our bonding ability and our aggressive parts are kept away from each other. A black and white hiding style can be a way to "cut off," or remove, parts of ourselves from others who would diminish us. Another example of splitting has to do with traumatic events that some people have experienced: splitting protects us from having to remember and reexperience traumatic events that would be too destructive to handle at the time. The antidote to splitting is reconciliation.

  —What splitting had Elaine done?

  — What splitting of either type, if any, have you done?

- **_Do-It-All Style (Perceived Omnipotence):_** In cases where trust has been hurt, we believe that we truly can exist without others' help. Complicating that illusion is the fact that we can quite often become extremely resourceful and competent at problem solving.

  — What had George's perceived omnipotence been hiding?

— In what aspects of your life, if any, are you feeling omnipotent? What might that sense be hiding?

- **Sour Grapes Style (Devaluation):** If we don't believe either that caring people exist or that we actually have a need to be cared for, we make our loneliness seem less painful. We minimize pain, for instance, by pretending that someone never mattered enough to us to hurt us.

  — What kind of devaluation did George do after his wife left him?

  — Think back over your own life. On what occasions, if any, have you devalued the significance of a loss? Be specific.

- **Hostility Style:** When individuals have experienced extreme detachment or their loving feelings have been punished in some way, they often develop reactive hostility. People who use rage protect themselves from more hurt by using anger to provide the illusion of power. This helps defend against having helpless, hurt, needy feelings.

  — When had George used defensive hostility?

  — When, if ever, have you used hostility to protect yourself from feeling or being vulnerable?

RELATIONAL HIDING FROM ATTACHMENT (PAGE 204)

Just as the internal styles hide us from our own needs for love, relationship styles paralyze us in isolation from those who would love us the most. Let's look at the most prominent of these styles. Be aware that people often have more than one relational hiding style.

- *The Lone Ranger Style (Detached):* Individuals with this hiding pattern exhibit lives that are simply empty of deep relationships. Their relational connections tend to be superficial or nonexistent. These individuals also seem to have no need for relationship.

    — What Lone Ranger, if any, have you known? What void in the heart do you think that hiding pattern was protecting?

    — Are you (or have you ever been) a Lone Ranger? What emptiness inside are you protecting?

- *The Hermit Style (Avoidant):* Similar to the detached style, avoidant people also move through life alone. The difference is that they are emotionally aware of their need for connection. Their attachment injury is very painful to them.

    — The problem for avoidant individuals is that *their fear of love is experienced as greater than their need for love.* When, if ever, have you known someone like this? A hint is that, when they begin to allow intimacy, they abruptly sabotage it or anxiously disconnect.

    — Are you (or have you ever been) avoidant? If so, what has caused you to fear love?

- **_The Rescuer Style (Caretaking):_** Often, people who have unmet attachment needs will take responsibility for the emotional needs of others. While these caretakers seem quite connected to others, the nature of their relationships is overwhelmingly one-way. It is as if they are always on the "giving" end because it is difficult for them to receive love.

  — What caretaker, if any, have you known? What habits (like Jane's "Fine-how-are-you-what-are-you-doing-today?") hinted at that person's struggle to receive love?

  — Are you (or have you ever been) a caretaker? Why do you find it difficult to receive love?

  — If you are concerned about whether you are codependent (enabling the irresponsibility of others), answer these two questions: Is what you are doing from a cheerful heart rather than from fear or guilt? Will your action help the person grow spiritually, instead of promoting sin or irresponsibility in him? A _yes_ answer to both questions means you are being loving rather than codependent.

- **_The Porcupine Style (Hostile Distancer):_** Using the internal hiding style of reactive hostility, hostile distancers keep people away by a chronic anger and mistrust that eventually may wear down the most persistently caring person.

  — What porcupine, if any, have you known? What caring people did you see that person wear down and push away?

— In projection, the distancer projects his own negative feelings into others, causing him to feel persecuted and attacked by others. Who in your life, if anyone, has been guilty of projection? Who was the target of that projection, and how did those people respond?

— When, if ever, have you been a hostile distancer? What was/is behind your anger and mistrust? And when, if ever, have you projected your fears onto someone else? What impact did that action have on the relationship?

- **Passive-Aggressive Style:** These individuals tend to be highly resentful of others' supposed control over them, but they don't directly confront them. Instead, they show their anger in indirect ways, such as procrastination, sarcastic humor, "forgetfulness," and intentional inefficiency.

  — Whom have you known whose passive-aggressive style kept them from admitting their rage at others? What indirect ways of showing their anger did they use?

  — In what relationship(s) are you (or have you been) passive-aggressive rather than being open about your anger? Did you show your anger through procrastination, sarcastic humor, "forgetfulness," intentional inefficiency, or another way?

- **Antisocial Styles:** In the antisocial pattern of relating, individuals live according to the law of the jungle: *every man for himself.* Antisocials see love only as weakness or vulnerability.

— With what antisocial person, if any, have you had contact? What evidence did you see of that person's inability to empathize, feel another's pain, or even conceptualize attachment?

— In what relationship(s), if any, would the other person see you as having an antisocial style? What evidence would that person give? In your possible defense, what is your attitude toward love?

- ***Addictive and Compulsive Styles:*** Addictions to, or compulsive behaviors concerning, substances, food, sex, or work are a character pattern for individuals with attachment deficits. The object of the addiction or compulsion becomes a substitute for relationship.

  — What was Michael's addiction? What vicious cycle did he create for himself?

  — What in your life, if anything, may be a substitute for relationship? What, if anything, are you addicted to or at least compulsive about?

JENNY'S HIDING FROM ATTACHMENT (PAGE 210)

Though our emotional "sentries" attempt to protect us from unloving people or other pains, they also keep us away from caring people and experiences that might heal and strengthen us. As we understand what the "sentries" protect, however, we can learn what developmental need is being automatically, and reactively, guarded. With that information, we can take steps to heal the injured part of the self.

Jenny's "sour grapes" and omnipotent defenses may be somewhat like your own. Like Jenny, the longer you hide, the more disconnected your emotions become. And the more you find yourself hiding behind some of the defenses we have looked at in this chapter, the more you should consider it a signal of the amount of pain you are facing.

- In what ways, if any, are you like Jenny?

- Look at the charts on pages 212–13 of the text. Review the recommended steps for moving away from "sour grapes" and omnipotent defenses and back toward relationship with God and others. Try one of the suggestions this week.

In the next chapter, we will turn to the second major developmental need in our lives—separateness—and the various styles of internal and external hiding that it triggers.

Coming Out of Hiding

1. Learning to discern your own specific tendencies to hide can give you important insight into your growth needs and whether you are defending a broken trusting part, an injured will, a hurt imperfect self, or a bruised authority need. First, consider your ability to trust God and others and to say yes to relationship. Look at the summary of Jenny's hiding patterns and the "Hiding from Attachment" block (pages 210–12 of the text). What causes (abandonment, abuse, detachment, superficial family intimacy, and so on), symptoms, and/or fears do you deal with?

2. Internal hiding styles are those patterns we use to hide from our painful feelings, thoughts, and memories. Relational hiding styles are consistent but problematic ways of interacting with people and tasks. Where, if at all, do you see yourself on the "Internal Hiding from Attachment" and "Relational Hiding from Attachment" charts (pages 212 and 213 of the text respectively)? Which internal hiding styles and which relational hiding styles does a trusted friend see in you? And what actions do you think you need to pursue to get free of those styles? Circle those actions and then choose one to work on this week.

3. Some actions that lead to freedom from hiding require a change of heart. Make those the focus of your prayer time. Also, since each of these actions will require courage and risk, ask God to guide you and give you boldness and a sense of his presence as you take these steps toward intimate relationship with him and others.

CHAPTER FOURTEEN

Hiding from Separateness
✛

Our second major developmental need is to become a person with will, boundaries, and an accurate sense of responsibility. This is our need for separateness.

- Our need for separateness can be damaged by relational experiences where either we say no to taking biblical responsibility for ourselves or we say yes to taking unbiblical responsibility for another person. When have you done one or the other or both? What damage (if any) to your need for separateness occurred?

- What damage (if any) to your need for separateness has resulted from enmeshment struggles, boundary failures, abuse, or parental failure to encourage separation?

The predominant fear of people with separateness deficits is that being separate will cause abandonment and isolation. The prospect of setting boundaries strikes terror that they will be forever alone. The fear of abandonment or isolation and the fear of being attacked for saying no compel them to create hiding patterns that help ensure the isolation of their need to make autonomous choices and judgments, set limits, and develop their "*no* muscle."

INTERNAL HIDING FROM SEPARATENESS (PAGE 216)

- *Log and Speck Style (Projection):* For the boundary-injured individual, aloneness is terrifying. What is projected, then, are the person's aggressive characteristics.

  — Joyce was afraid of her own hostile parts. So how did she deal with her anger?

  — To stand against others on principle, to be righteously angry, or to refuse to tolerate the irresponsibility of another person are all aggressive parts of being created in the image of God. Comment on how comfortable you are with these parts of you, if you are even in touch with them.

- *Emotional Picture Style (Introjection):* The person struggling with separateness issues takes on others' characteristics of closeness, but without boundaries. In other words, they will form a mental image of a relationship with continuous and endless nurturance. They emotionally swim in an ocean of fusion with the other person.

  — Why wasn't Sue's introjection satisfying?

  — What emotional and idealistic pictures keep you from connecting to people in a healthy, real way?

- **Black and White Style (Splitting):** Boundary-deficient people often use splitting to keep love and limits apart. They fear that their rage will overwhelm and destroy their loving, tender feelings. So they keep appropriate anger and responsible boundaries away from their caring parts.

  — Feeling that conflict meant hate, what splitting had Burt done?

  — What is your attitude toward conflict, and what is your usual emotional response to it? Avoiding conflict can keep us from speaking the truth in love. When have you had the opportunity to speak the truth in love? Did you? Why or why not?

- **Do-It-All Style (Perceived Omnipotence):** Often, separateness-injured individuals will believe they can keep others happy, or content, or loving. This sort of omnipotence keeps them from the disturbing truth that anyone can leave them at any time.

  — What power over her father did Trudy think she had? What efforts in futility resulted?

  — When, if ever, have you tried hard to keep someone happy, content, or loving? Talk about your efforts and their results.

- **Self-Attacking Style (Turning Against the Self):** In this style of internal hiding from separateness, the aggression that can't be "owned" is redirected against the self. It becomes more acceptable to hate ourselves than to tell the truth about our rage at the sin of others against us.

— What prompted Tom's justifiable rage, and how did he deal with it?

— When, if ever, have you been angry but punished the safest target: yourself? Describe the situation as well as a scenario showing a healthier way to channel your anger.

- **Safe Target Style (Displacement):** The "safe target" style occurs when the fear of confronting another person causes us to attack or criticize someone who isn't as threatening. We are not concealing our aggressive parts; we are concealing the target at which they are actually aimed.

  — In light of this definition, explain what is going on when the office worker goes home and kicks the dog.

  — When, if ever, have you, figuratively speaking, kicked the dog? What was the actual target of your anger? What would have been a healthier alternative?

- **Undoing:** Undoing is based on the assumption that there is actually something we can do to negate or annul something destructive we do, say, or think. The undoer believes that compliance can erase badness.

  — What undoing did I attempt when I was six years old?

— What undoing, if any, have you attempted in your life? Be specific about both the destructive action, words, or thoughts you were trying to undo and how you attempted to do that. What would have been a healthier approach?

- **Regression Style:** Regression is a hiding style that returns the individual to an earlier stage of immaturity. Regression can occur in the form of emotional breakdowns, relational conflicts, impulsivity, and disruptions in carrying out responsibilities. People who struggle with defensive regression are convinced, at some level, that the only way they can have relationships is to be childish around others.

  — What was behind Laura's regression? Consider the timing of the regression.

  — When, if ever, has a season of change or loss triggered some regression in you? What is the difference between authentic and defensive regressions, and which regression did you experience?

RELATIONAL HIDING FROM SEPARATENESS (PAGE 222)

- **Caretaking Style:** As well as protecting us against having needy attachment feelings, caretaking can do "double duty" as a defense against being separate. The caretaker has a built-in guarantee of relationship of some sort. Though it is rarely the kind of attachment that actually nurtures the caretaker, in the caretaker's eyes it beats being alone.

  — What caretaker, if any, have you known? What did you see happen when that person began asking for what she or he was giving?

— Are you (or have you ever been) a caretaker? Explain how caretaking is a kind of control and why the result for the caretaker is compliance rather than love.

- **Dependence Style:** Dependent people hide from their responsible, willing, choosing parts. They fear that if they make their own choices, others will leave them. So they relate to others like a child to a parent.

  — So frightened of aloneness, dependent individuals will go to almost any lengths to keep others close by. When have you seen someone compromise principles, give up freedoms, or submit to manipulation in order to maintain a relationship and not be alone? Be specific about the price that person paid to keep another close by.

  — When, if ever, have you compromised your principles, given up freedoms, or submitted to manipulation in order to maintain a relationship and not be alone? What hints, if any, did you have that the person with whom you were in relationship was motivated more by feelings of obligation and guilt rather than by love?

- **Victim Style:** In this relating pattern, individuals approach relationships from a position of blaming others. They see their own unhappiness and circumstances as the fault of others and tend to look for others to take responsibility to repair their injuries. This victim style denies the autonomy, choices, power, and responsibility of the victim.

— A victim is someone who has been injured in order to satisfy the evil purpose of another. When have you seen a victim fall into a victim style of relating? What re-victimization occurred? In contrast, when, if ever, have you seen a victim differentiate between "fault for the injury" (the perpetrator's part) and "responsibility to heal" (the victim's own part)? Note how the victim's willingness to take responsibility to heal made (or would have made) a difference in his or her relationships.

— Does confrontation feel like blame and condemnation to you? Do you have a victim style that prevents you from being able to hear truth spoken in love and still feel loved? Support your yes or no answer with details about how you have handled a specific confrontation.

- **Manipulation Style:** People with a manipulative character pattern use others to avoid taking responsibility for their own lives. Rather than being able to undergo the training of learning God's law of consequences, manipulators may use any or all of several tactics to avoid responsibility.

  — When have you seen manipulators not respect other people's boundaries; coerce others; ask others to bail them out of jams; continually borrow money from others; use people in indirect ways without actually asking for help; or take "shortcuts" to responsibility by, for instance, being deceptive with others about time or money or by making people who say no to them feel guilty?

— When, if ever, have you manipulated others by not respecting other people's boundaries; coercing others; asking others to bail you out of jams; continually borrowing money from others; using people in indirect ways without actually asking for help; or taking "shortcuts" to responsibility by, for instance, being deceptive with others about time or money or by making people who say no to you feel guilty? Why did you choose to manipulate that person?

- **Chaotic Style:** This character pattern tends to be impulsive, disorganized, and directionless. This person's needs for connection will draw him or her toward others in a dependent fashion, but the connection cannot be sustained, and the person distances by isolation or impulsive behavior.

  — When have you seen someone relate to another (perhaps to you) in this kind of chaotic style? Why was that person unable to stay connected: because the person she got close to disappointed her and was therefore "all bad," or because her own fears of closeness caused her to protect herself by sabotaging the closeness?

  — When, if ever, have you adopted a chaotic style of relating? Give a few details about your impulsiveness, disorganization, or directionlessness in that relationship. Also state why you were not able to stay connected: Did the person you got close to disappoint you, or did you protect yourself by sabotaging the closeness?

- **Passive-Aggressive Style:** Passive-aggressiveness keeps attachment-injured individuals from risking closeness and separateness-injured individuals from feelings of aloneness. This style punishes supposedly controlling people but protects these individuals from having to take responsibility for the aggressive feelings they have toward others.

— Vance's wife began to clearly see his passive-aggressive style when he turned off the oven and ruined her soufflé. When have you seen a person's passive-aggressive style emerge? Be specific about his or her actions.

— When, if ever, have you been passive-aggressive in an attempt to not feel alone and/or to avoid taking responsibility for aggressive feelings you had toward another? What impact did your style have on the relationship?

- **Histrionic Style:** The histrionic pattern has three basic characteristics: a deep sense of dependency; seductiveness with the opposite sex to meet the dependency need; and negative feelings toward the opposite sex for being "seduceable."

  — Individuals with this hiding style "live for" romance. Their lives feel empty if there is no romance occurring. Who among your friends and acquaintances fits this description? Explain your choice with details from his or her life.

  — Is your style of relating histrionic? Support your answer with details about your dating or relating history. How does romance protect you personally from having to embrace loneliness and independence?

- **Addictive and Compulsive Styles:** Just as dependencies on food, substances, and sex help people hide from closeness, addictions and compulsions also protect them from being alone. Addicts often use a substance in order to regain their sense of attachment and warmth that, for some reason, they don't find readily available in relationships.

— When have you seen someone use food, substances, or sex as protection from being alone? What suggested to you that this addiction was replacing connection with people?

— When, if ever, have you used food, substances, or sex to protect yourself from being alone? If you are not still on that path, what helped you change direction? If you sense you are on that path, what might you do to change courses?

JENNY'S SEPARATENESS (PAGE 229)

Jenny lived the nightmare of the person hiding from separateness: abandonment and isolation. Even though Jenny knew the external circumstances that had forced her away from her parents, the separation injury was so great that she looked for internal reasons to explain why her parents had been taken away from her. She convinced herself that her parents' capture was somehow her fault, and she fell into self-hatred. Fortunately, Officer Josef's love stepped in to help her before it was too late.

• Like Jenny, are you engaging in self-attack? Describe it and also try to trace its roots, as done above in Jenny's case.

• As a result of your separateness, are you seeing yourself as either more spiritual or guiltier than you truly are? From what does this perspective protect you?

• Now consider taking some risks. Check to see if you may be holding on to anger about some personal injustice or injury. Find some safe relationships and turn toward God's faithful loving-kindness to better understand your own hiding.

In the next chapter, we will try to identify which hiding patterns we develop when we experience injuries to our souls that keep us from understanding the good and bad in ourselves.

Coming Out of Hiding

1. Our second major developmental need is to become a person with will, boundaries, an accurate sense of responsibility, and the ability to say no. This is our need for separateness. Look again at the summary of Jenny's hiding pattern and the "Hiding from Separateness" block (pages 229–30 of the text). What causes (enmeshment struggles, boundary failures, abuse, parental failure to encourage separation, and so on), symptoms, and/or fears do you deal with?

2. Where, if at all, do you see yourself on the charts "Internal Hiding from Separateness" and "Relational Hiding from Separateness" (pages 230 and 231 of the text respectively)? Which internal hiding styles and which relational hiding styles does a trusted friend see in you? What actions do you think you need to pursue to get free of those styles? Circle those actions and then choose one to work on this week.

3. Some actions that lead to freedom from hiding require a change of heart. Make those the focus of your prayer time. Also ask God to show you how you protect yourself from being separate and to guide you to some safe relationships that can point you to his faithful loving-kindness and a better understanding of your own hiding.

CHAPTER FIFTEEN

Hiding from Our Good and Bad Selves

✥

Attachment and separateness define the existence of our soul. Good/ bad deficits and authority conflicts help determine the quality of life of our soul. Because of their importance to the functioning of our soul, it helps to understand how we hide from God's love in these two areas. In this chapter we will deal with hiding from our good and bad selves.

RESOLVING GOOD AND BAD (PAGE 234)

We need to accept the bad parts of ourselves and the world. This need is important, because it helps us bring our own badness to a place of forgiveness. Our imperfect characteristics need to be brought into connection with God and others.

- Share an early memory of facing and having to accept a bad part of the world. What happened and how did you respond?

- Likewise, share an early memory of facing and having to accept a part of yourself. What characteristic did you have to acknowledge, and why was that either hard or not so hard?

Our "forgiveness muscle" can be injured in many ways: a perfectionistic environment or one in which failure is a cause for shame; relationships and families that overstress the "excellent" parts of people at the expense of the "mediocre" parts; overpositive environments that keep us from legitimate grief; and families who keep members stuck in a naïve position.

- Which of these ways, if any, of denying one's bad parts have you encountered? Give a few details.

- Which of these ways of injuring a forgiveness muscle and encouraging denial of one's bad parts might you be propagating in your own home? What might you do to stop that trend?

The predominant fear of individuals who are injured in their ability to resolve goodness and badness is that badness will annihilate goodness. These people are afraid that if they admit bad parts in themselves or others, they or others will forever be stuck in an "all bad," or hated, position.

INTERNAL HIDING FROM BADNESS (PAGE 234)

As we have seen, we hide in two basic patterns: *internally*, in which we hide from painful internal feelings, thoughts, or memories; and externally or *relationally*, in which we develop problematic ways of dealing with people and tasks. First, let's look at internal ways we hide from our sinfulness and our perceived badness.

- ***The "Log and Speck" Style (Projection):*** Terrified of being found out or exposed in their imperfections, forgiveness-injured individuals reject those characteristics of themselves that they consider imperfect and unconsciously place them on others.

  — Why was Brenda impatient with Nancy? Which of her own characteristics was Brenda rejecting and unconsciously placing on Nancy?

— What characteristics of yourself, if any, are you projecting on some-one? Be specific about the what, the who, and how your projection affects your relationship with that person.

- *Emotional Picture Style (Introjection):* People with good-bad deficits have taken inside themselves a distorted image of what people should be. The emotional picture becomes one of two extremes: either an "all-good" or an "all-bad" picture of themselves.

  — What picture of himself had Martin introjected? Why did that keep him hiding from his high school classmates?

  — What distorted image of yourself do you have? Are you either "all good" or "all bad" in your own eyes? What have been some of the consequences of this introjection?

- *Black and White Style (Splitting):* Probably more than any other developmental injury, black and white thinking dominates people with good-bad deficits. These individuals have not experienced sufficient grace to be assured that they will not lose attachment if their faults are "exposed."

  — What splitting had Colleen done? What happened in the support group for other bulimic women that helped her begin to accept this destruc-tive behavior as part of herself?

  — What splitting, if any, have you done? What faults are you afraid of having exposed? Where might you find grace and acceptance?

- **Do-It-All Style (Perceived Omnipotence):** The good-bad deficient individual often maintains a false feeling of power over his or her badness. This power shows itself in two ways: "I can successfully hide my badness" and "By hiding my badness, I can eliminate it." But we are powerless to "will" away our faults without relationship (specifically without relationship with Christ [Romans 6:15–8:1]), and we can't conceal our bad parts perfectly because they will be exposed by their fruits.

  — When, if ever, have you seen someone try to eliminate their shameful parts by various omnipotent methods: willpower, discipline, self-denial, trying harder, looking at the "bright side"? What method(s) did that person use? Did that person ever start accepting limitations and recognize his or her need for grace?

  — When, if ever, have you tried to eliminate your shameful parts by various omnipotent methods: willpower, discipline, self-denial, trying harder, looking at the "bright side"? What method(s) did you use? What steps might you take toward beginning to accept your limitations and thereby recognize your need for grace?

- **Peak-to-Pits Style (Idealization-Devaluation):** Individuals who need to avoid experiencing badness defend themselves by finding others on whom they can project perfection. When they find the perfect person, idealizers then place all their hopes and dreams on that individual. Then, when the depravity or immaturity of the idealized other finally comes out, the idealizer becomes terribly disappointed and hurt by the "betrayal" of the other.

  — When have you or someone you know not noticed the humanness of a friend? (That humanness always includes sin and badness.) What happened to the relationship when that humanness could not be ignored?

  — Who, if anyone, are you currently idealizing? Take two or three minutes to try to list that person's negative qualities. Also, in a sentence or two, state why this exercise is worthwhile.

- *Soapbox Style (Reaction Formation):* Related to the projection style, soapbox hiding creates a passion against the "bad" part of the self we are concealing. This passion erupts in our personal vendettas or pet peeves. The result is that we react in an opposite direction to that bad part of ourselves.

  — What bad part of himself was Sam hiding? What opposite activity, iron- ically, was Sam's good part doing?

  — What is a personal vendetta or pet peeve for you? What does this pas- sion you just identified suggest about the "bad" part you are concealing?

RELATIONAL HIDING FROM BADNESS (PAGE 240)

- *The Perfectionist Style:* Perfectionists experience one failure as total failure. They desperately try to keep good and bad apart by harsh and self- critical expectations of themselves that no one could achieve.

  — What expectations for herself did Elizabeth have? What was her response when she didn't meet those expectations during her spring recital?

  — What harsh and self-critical expectations of yourself— expectations that no one could achieve—do you have? When you fail, what is your response? Where might you go to find a safety net of grace?

- *The Admiration Addict Style:* One style that attempts to hide badness presents a grandiose, "superstar" self to others, which is designed to draw attention to the person's strengths and conceal the person's perceived weaknesses. Yet, driven by a deep sense of shame, the admiration addict is continually in dread that he or she will be "found out" and exposed as a fraud.

— What comment by a group member pointed out the degree of Jim's addiction to admiration? What happened that helped him lose his taste for admiration?

—Are you addicted to admiration—or do you know someone who is? Wh strengths do you or that person work hard to draw attention to? If you are an admiration addict, what is the cause of the deep sense of shame driving your effort to hide your perceived weaknesses?

• **The Pollyanna Style:** This style refers to a tendency of some good-bad injured individuals to look only at the good side of themselves and others. They take a naïve and idealistic view of life, expecting the best of it without being prepared for disappointment. Often, they come from homes in which badness wasn't discussed frankly and lovingly.

— Think of a one-time Pollyanna you may have known. What distorted thoughts (listed on page 244 of the text) guided that person's think- ing? What event forced that person to acknowledge his or her own or other people's self-centered and destructive parts?

— What Pollyanna thinking, if any, have you done? Give a specific exam- ple or two. What distorted thoughts (page 244), if any, did you grow up with? And what event in your life forced you to admit that you, or others, have self-centered and destructive parts? What was your emo- tional reaction to that truth?

• **The Romantic Style:** Like the Pollyanna, the romantic looks at only good things, but with a particular focus: Life is built on the excitement and passion of romantic love. This person can endure anything as long as he or she has an intense, emotional involvement in a dating relationship or with a spouse.

— What romantic, if any, have you known? How far along Sharon's path was that person?

— Do you have a romantic hiding style? If so, what convinced you that you are fundamentally boring and have nothing interesting to say besides passionate exchanges? Where can you go to find deep, abiding, and healing Christian love?

- **The All-or-Nothing Style:** The all-or-nothing style reflects an undeveloped ability to tolerate good and bad to the extent that relationships become almost impossible. It is as if there is no place in the person's head for both traits to exist. The thinking can be, "When you agree with me, you're good. When you disagree with me, you must not understand me, so you're bad." This split happens within as well: If the all-or-nothing person feels loved, he or she feels "good." If there is conflict or frustration in the relationship, the all-or-nothing person often will experience himself or herself as "bad."

  — Who in your life, if anyone, does this description remind you of? What kind of connection do, or did, you have with that person?

  — In what details (if any) of the description above do you see yourself? Is it easier for you to accept bad in others or in yourself? Why might that be the case—and what will you do about it?

- **Addictions and Compulsions:** As we have noted in previous stages, out-of-control behaviors, thoughts, and feelings are also protective. These habits keep the good-bad injured individual from the shame of experiencing perceived bad parts.

— What did the compulsive shopper learn about herself when she looked at the timing of her sprees?

— What addictions or compulsions, if any, keep you from experiencing your perceived bad parts?

HIDING FROM EVIL, SEARCHING FOR TRUTH (PAGE 246)

Now we have looked at the problem of human nature: Each of us is created in God's image, yet each of us has a sinful nature. The practical problem is "What do I do with my actual and my perceived badness?" Sometimes we deal with it constructively and come out of hiding. Sometimes we treat it in destructive ways and push ourselves deeper into the Deep Woods.

- If we try to hide our imperfections, we will end up in the self-deception and hatred that Jenny fell into when she first attacked herself through Big Jenny. But if we deny that goodness resides in us, we will believe the lie that Little Jenny started absorbing. Where, if at all, do you see yourself in this description of Big Jenny and Little Jenny? Be specific about times and reasons you have attacked yourself (if you have done that) and/or lies about yourself that you have absorbed.

- Using King David as your example, describe the path toward acceptance of the bad. What parts do confession and repentance play in gaining and maintaining spiritual and psychological health? About what do you need to be honest before God?

- Now consider taking some risks. Check to see if you are holding deeply felt anger about some personal injustice or injury. Find some safe relationships and turn toward God's faithful loving-kindness to better understand your own hiding.

Accept yourself for who you are—a person created in God's image, capable of noble and selfless deeds, but also a person who is sinful, imperfect, and unfinished. And remember that, as we accept God himself through Christ, we receive the grace that he bestows through forgiveness. Along with this unmerited acceptance and restoration, he also provides people of grace who can come alongside us and flesh out for us in our daily lives the reality of his forgiveness and love.

Coming Out of Hiding

1. Attachment and separateness define the existence of our soul; good-bad deficits and authority conflicts determine the quality of life of our soul. Consider now how you hide from maturing your good and bad selves and how your "forgiveness muscle" has been injured. Look again at the summary of Jenny's hiding patterns and the "Hiding from Resolving Good and Bad" block (pages 246–48 of the text). What causes (a perfectionistic environment; relationships and families that overstress the "excellent" parts of people; overpositive environments that keep us from legitimate grief; idealistic denial; and so on), symptoms, and/or fears do you deal with?

2. Where, if at all, do you see yourself on the charts "Internal Hiding from Our Good and Bad Selves" and "Relational Hiding from Our Good and Bad Selves" (pages 248 and 249 of the text respectively)? Which internal hiding styles and which relationship hiding styles does a trusted friend see in you? What actions do you think you need to pursue to get free of those styles? Circle those actions and then choose one to work on this week.

3. Some actions that lead to freedom from hiding require a change of heart. Make those the focus of your prayer time. Also ask God to shine the light of his healing truth and grace on the needy, immature parts of your soul as you move on to the next-to-last chapter and its suggestions about how to resolve your hiding dilemmas.

CHAPTER SIXTEEN

Hiding from Authority and Adulthood

✣

O ur fourth spiritual and emotional developmental need is to establish a biblical sense of our own adulthood and authority. When this part of our character remains undeveloped, it is often due to improper use of authority in the home.

- Think about the home you grew up in. Would you describe the authority as too strict (authoritarianism), too lenient (laissez-faire parenting), or inconsistent (a combination of both styles)? Refer to specific incidents to support your answer.

- Individuals who have authority injuries often experience a basic fear of being attacked or criticized for taking adult authority over their lives. They sometimes become approval seekers, and they generally hide from either aggressive or sexual parts of themselves. Exposing aggression or sexuality could, they think, bring on criticism by a parental figure. Which of these injuries, if any, did you experience due to your parents' parenting style?

As with the other three primary areas of our soul already examined, authority-injured people exhibit two general hiding patterns—internal and relational.

INTERNAL HIDING FROM ADULT AUTHORITY (PAGE 252)

- **Shoving Underneath Style (Repression):** With this defense mechanism, we attempt to remove intolerable thoughts and feelings by sending them out of our consciousness. An authority deficiency makes us fearful of displeasing those we see as adult. As a result, when we become aware of parts of ourselves that might bring on disapproval, we shove those parts underneath our consciousness in order to forget them.

  — Remember the woman who suffered from sexual inhibition (page 252 of the text)? What contributed to that, and what did her repression look like?

  — What intolerable thoughts and feelings, if any, might you be avoiding? What adult authority are you afraid of displeasing? What might be the roots of both the repression and the fear that you will bring on another person's disapproval?

- **Soapbox Style (Reaction Formation):** Just as individuals with good-bad conflicts employ this hiding style, it is also commonly found among authority-injured people. They develop an opposite reaction that hides them from a threatening adult part of the soul.

  — What reaction did Paul have to authority? What true feelings toward authority was that reaction hiding?

— What reaction formation may you be hiding behind? What true attitudes toward authority are behind that reaction? What threatening adult part of your soul might you be trying to avoid by reacting in a way totally opposite of what you feel?

- **Erasing Style (Undoing):** "Undoing" attempts to negate our supposed destructiveness. We use erasing as an emotional sentry to try to make up for our rebellious feelings by behaving in artificially loving ways toward others. Undoing is based on a fear that there is not enough forgiveness to allow us to be pardoned and an omnipotent fantasy that we can erase our mistakes.

  — Think about Scott. What behavior was he using to try to erase his guilt over feeling angry with an employee?

  — What rebellious or negative feelings do you try to erase with artificially loving actions? Be specific about both the actions and the feelings behind them.

- **Intellectualization Style:** When authority-deficient people are afraid of assuming their own adult position, they often retreat to their head (logical thinking) instead of their heart (dealing with emotions). The goal of intellectualizers is to stay away from feelings that might cause them to do or say something offensive. Often this hiding style protects them from intense sadness, longing, or hostility.

  — When intellectualizers are asked how they feel, they generally respond with an opinion. What intellectualizer, if any, have you known? What indications did you have that that person was trying to avoid his or her feelings?

— To what degree, if any, are you an intellectualizer? What sadness, desire, or hostility might you be trying to avoid—and how are you doing that?

- *Guilt Style:* Guilt feelings are self-condemning emotions that cause us to criticize ourselves for real or perceived wrongdoing. These guilt feelings can become a hiding style for the authority-injured person, because guilt is generally anger turned inward. (In contrast, godly sorrow is authentic remorse for being unloving toward another.)

  — Who among your friends and acquaintances seems to hide behind guilt? What evidence of self-criticism do you see in his or her words and actions?

  — Do you habitually criticize yourself for real or perceived wrongdoing? What might be behind this anger turned inward on yourself?

- *Excusing Style (Rationalization):* This commonly used hiding pattern confuses "reasons" for "justifications." Authority-injured persons will often find excuses for their impulsive words or actions, which are in actuality used to prevent the anger of another toward them. Instead of providing reasons for their actions, they instead offer excuses in hopes of averting the anger of the parental person. Also, people who hide with rationalizations are fearful of taking responsibility for their seemingly dangerous traits.

  — What rationalization did Jackie use when she dropped out of medical school? What was she hiding from?

— When, if ever, have you hidden behind excuses to avoid someone's anger? Be specific about the situation. Is this excusing a pattern in your life? If so, what seemingly dangerous traits are you afraid to take responsibility for?

• ***Non-Medical Medical Problems (Somatization):*** At times, authority-injured persons will develop pains and symptoms (back and head pain, abdominal problems, sexual difficulties) that have no medical basis. The body gets sick when the person is in a position to grow up in some area. The physical ailment keeps the focus off the spiritual and relational issue.

— Explain what was going on with Toni's headaches.

— Is somatization a pattern in your life? What physical ailment recurs? What spiritual and/or relational issue might it be distracting you from?

RELATIONAL HIDING FROM AUTHORITY (PAGE 257)

• ***The Approval-Seeking Child Style:*** People in an approval-seeking position are afraid of breaking rules and tend to be overly careful, obsessed with making "right decisions." They have a hard time seeing themselves as adults without having to find a "parent" to approve of their decisions.

— When, if ever, has your desire for approval made it hard for you to make a decision? Be specific. Do you see in your life a pattern of approval seeking?

— Jesus taught that whenever tradition, or human rules, break with God's, we are to "obediently rebel." This is why many families get worse before they get better when they finally decide to deal with emotional issues. When, if ever, have you seen a family get worse before it got better? Who in the family got worse as one member tried to get healthy?

- **The Controlling Parent Style:** Often an authority conflict doesn't emerge in a life as a "one-down" or childish perspective. It comes out more as being "one-up," or parental of others. The person with this style has learned to identify with controlling figures to avoid challenging them.

  — Reintroduce yourself to Phil, whom you met at the beginning of chapter 7. With whom was he the controlling parent? And which controlling figures was he not challenging?

  — When, if ever, have you adopted the controlling parent style? Do you report never having had a "questioning" or rebellious period in your life? Are you judgmental of other people who represent the split-off adolescent in your own heart?

- **The Rebellious Child Style:** Rebels question and challenge whether the authority they are under is legitimate or not. They don't have the ability to experience authority as constructive. And, like the child and parental positions, rebels also feel like a child around adults. Their rebellion is not freedom, because it is simply a reaction to control. It is not being an adult.

  — Why do people in the rebellious child position tend to job hunt a great deal?

— What is your usual reaction to authority? When, if ever, have you rebelled? In what situations have you struggled to see authority as constructive?

- ***Obsessive-Compulsive Style:*** This character pattern tends to be unduly conventional, authority-bound, more comfortable with tasks than relationships, and has trouble making decisions. Quite often, the obsessive's preoccupation with details keeps him or her from arriving at larger-scale decisions that urgently need to be made.

  — Who among your friends and acquaintances would you label "obsessive-compulsive"? What habits and rituals are an important part of that person's daily life?

  — To what degree, if any, are you obsessive-compulsive? What habits and rituals help you feel more in control of your life? Which of the following situations (each of which calls for you to take control of your life) might you be avoiding: confronting a superior, changing jobs, requesting a favor from someone, or something else?

- ***Addictive and Compulsive Styles:*** Substance abuse, overeating, overspending, sexual impulsiveness, and compulsive habits serve authority-deficient individuals by providing a place for their rebellious parts to emerge. This behavior is a disguised form of rebellion and is usually seen as uncharacteristic of the person. Yet such persons stay subservient with these episodes of "uncharacteristic" destructive behavior.

  — When have you seen an addictive/compulsive style seem uncharacteristic for the person acting out?

— What uncharacteristic addictive or compulsive behavior (if any) may be providing a place for your rebellious parts to emerge?

JENNY AND AUTHORITY (PAGE 264)

Fear of assuming authority is the starting point for many hiding patterns.

- Review the description of Jenny (page 264 of the text). In what ways do her experiences mirror your own? Be specific about what you have in common with Jenny.

- If we continue in the sort of harmful hiding patterns we have looked at in this chapter, our souls will, like Jenny's, become diminished. Our needy, immature parts will begin to atrophy for want of God's healing truth and grace. What sense do you have, if any, that this might be happening to you?

Let's turn now to the final chapter that will help you resolve your hiding dilemma. Here we seek the key to opening the door of the heart without further injuring what lies within.

Coming Out of Hiding

1. Our fourth spiritual and emotional development need is to establish a biblical sense of our own adulthood and authority. Consider now how you hide from those aspects of yourself and how you relate to the authority of other people. Look again at the "Hiding from Authority and Adulthood" block and the summary of Jenny's hiding patterns (pages 262 and 264–65 of the text respectively). What causes (too strict authority, too lenient authority, or inconsistent authority in the home), symptoms, and/or fears do you deal with?

2. Where, if at all, do you see yourself on the charts "Internal Hiding from Authority and Adulthood" and "Relational Hiding from Authority and Adulthood" (pages 262 and 263 of the text respectively)? Which internal hiding styles and which relational hiding styles does a trusted friend see in you? What actions do you think you need to pursue to get free of those styles? Circle those actions and then choose one to work on this week.

3. Some actions that lead to freedom from hiding require a change of heart. Make those the focus of your prayer time. Also, ask God to show you how you protect yourself from being separate and to guide you to some safe relationships that can point you to his faithful loving-kindness and a better understanding of your own hiding.

CHAPTER SEVENTEEN

Coming Out of Hiding

✤

In this final chapter, we will look at ways we can move out of our positions and styles of hiding. Whatever hiding patterns we commonly use, and whatever injured and undeveloped parts of the self we are trying to protect, God desires us to be free from the isolation of our souls (Luke 4:18–19). He has provided the resources to work through these patterns.

REMEMBERING WHY WE HIDE (PAGE 268)

It is an important step to be able to identify the defense mechanisms and character styles we use. Yet simply knowing our hiding patterns isn't enough for spiritual maturity to take place (1 Corinthians 8:1).

- What hiding patterns have you identified as you have worked through the text and this workbook?

Identification of our hiding patterns is the step that precedes other equally important steps: understanding the meaning of our hiding patterns, what needs they meet, what they protect, and what to do about them.

TWO INCOMPLETE SOLUTIONS (PAGE 269)

Harmful hiding patterns keep us from the very resources God has provided for our healing: grace, love (relationship), and truth. But too often we try to take shortcuts to healing, and we are going to look at two common shortcuts now.

- ***Confrontation Without Relationship:*** In this truth-without-love solution, the individual is told about his or her hiding patterns, but the confronter gives little thought to connecting in a personal way with the one confronted.

  — People who have developed long-term, safe, loving relationships can hear criticisms from their loved ones that might be quite wounding were they given by a mere acquaintance. When, if ever, has someone confronted you without having established a relationship and thus earned the right? What prompted the confrontation, and how did you react?

  — When, if ever, have you confronted a person without establishing a relationship and thus earning the right? What prompted your confronting, and how did the person react?

  — One of the two fruits of the confrontation-minus-relationship approach is *external compliance and an increase in hiding patterns*. Individuals who are excessively "truthed" often learn to pretend to be receptive to the information, but the injuries remain unhealed. *Open resentfulness and loss of relationship* is the other possible fruit. We sense that we are being pushed into an encounter that we are not ready for, and we react to protect ourselves. Which of these fruits has been (or do you think would be) the result of confrontation-minus-relationship in your life? Try to explain why.

- **_Relationship Without Confrontation:_** The problem with the relationship-without-truth approach is that grace minus truth leads to license or irresponsibility. Without a sense of our own responsibility to take active steps to heal our immaturities, growth becomes paralyzed (Romans 5:20–6:2).

  — When, if ever, has someone offered you a loving relationship but not confronted you about sin in your life? What greater benefit would you have received if that person had, in love, spoken truth to you?

  — When, if ever, have you offered someone love without confronting that person about sin in his or her life? Why did you withhold the truth? What benefit did the person receive from you? What greater benefit could that person you were in relationship with have enjoyed if you had confronted him or her in love?

  — While the love-minus-confrontation approach does help us step forth from our hiding place, quite often one of three distortions occurs: blaming (permanently focusing on the injustices of the other person), assuming a helpless position (we see ourselves as powerless and unable to do anything to solve our injuries), and apathy (this occurs when we are not aware of the cost of being forgiven; some call this "cheap grace"). Which of these fruits has been (or do you think would be) the result of relationship-minus-confrontation in your life? Try to explain why.

A DIFFERENT SOLUTION (PAGE 274)

Typically, the church has been identified with the "truth only" solution for hiding, and psychotherapy with the "grace only" approach. The truth is that both groups have excesses on either side.

- "Truth only" causes guilty concealment, and "grace only" causes irresponsible openness. When, if ever, have you found yourself guiltily concealing some part of you because you were confronted but not loved? Or when, if ever, have you found yourself being irresponsibly open because you were loved but not confronted with the truth? In those situations, what would you have appreciated receiving from the confronter-without-love or the lover-without-confrontation?

- Review the hiding patterns you have noticed in yourself. Now read below the list of what God has for you, circle what you think you most need, and then pray, asking God to give you courage as you open yourself to receiving that gift:

For those who have been hurt in the area of attachment, he wants to provide safe, loving relationships in which we can learn how to trust.

For those with deficiencies in separateness, he wants to help us learn how to repair our injured "*no* muscle."

For those who keep goodness and badness split apart, he wants to help us find places of forgiveness for ourselves and others and a realistic understanding of a fallen world.

For those who struggle with "one-down" positions, God wants to expose us to opportunities to become adults.

We are not able to change the past in which we were injured, but we can reach into the past to find and repair those frozen parts of our character.

STEPS TO A LIFE BEYOND HIDING (PAGE 276)

The following sequence of steps can lead us out of hiding. The key point to remember is that *the solution to hiding is simply removing our self-protective defenses; the solution is to make the defense unnecessary.* We accomplish that goal by meeting the need that the defense is protecting.

1. *Use your hiding pattern as a road map to your needs.* Defensive styles are a directional arrow for us. Remember the principle of opposites: you always react in a different way than the part under protection.

   — What spiritual and emotional needs do your hiding patterns point to? To help answer that question, ask trusted friends, "Do you see me doing this when I seem to be having a problem?"

2. *Actively seek confessional relationships.* Relationship is the soil from which grace can enter the injured self. We need to find safe relationships in which the immature parts of our soul can begin to emerge and where we can confess our sins or the sins of others against us. To confess is to allow others to see the part of us that we fear, hate, or are ashamed of. Whatever is unconfessed is beyond the reach of healing. The isolated injury that stays hidden feels "bad." The injury that is connected feels loved.

   — What part of you do you need to confess and allow others to see? Before speaking it aloud to someone, practice sharing here on paper the part of you that you fear, hate, or are ashamed of.

   — Next, review the nine characteristics of safe people (listed on pages 277–79 of the text). (For a more thorough discussion, see *Safe People: How to Find Relationships That Are Good for You and Avoid Those That Aren't* by Dr. Henry Cloud and Dr. John Townsend [Zondervan, 1995].) Who in your life, if anyone at this point, meets these criteria closely enough (perfection is not required) to help you heal? If you can't think of anyone, where will you go to start developing relationships with safe people?

3. *Take responsibility for developing the skills needed for repair.* Actively pursue the skills dealing with your specific developmental injuries (see chapters 4 through 7).

— Turn to the chapters that address your injuries. List the skills you need to develop and begin jotting down ideas about how you will work on developing those skills.

4. *Let go of outgrown hiding patterns.* Once we have repaired the deficits that caused the defenses, we no longer need the defenses. Losing hiding patterns often takes work, humility, and asking others for help to let go of defenses we no longer need.

— What struggle to let go of your outgrown hiding patterns do you anticipate? Make that struggle a topic of prayer.

5. *Maintain helpful hiding patterns.* Use appropriate hiding patterns to keep yourself connected yet protected. Don't be vulnerable with someone who opposes your attempts to stop hiding. Helpful hiding styles such as boundaries, anticipation, humor, and patience will continue to be necessary.

— Review chapters 8 and 9 so that you are well aware of helpful hiding styles. Which ones do you need to strengthen for your healing journey? What will you do toward that end?

6. *Learn to give what you have received.* As we are restored, repaired, and matured, we are to help others find the same help we have found. This is both a responsibility and a natural outgrowth of being loved.

— Think about people already in your life who are helping you along this path toward freedom from hiding. In what ways are they giving what they have received? What do you look forward to being able to do in the way of giving what you will receive as you are restored, repaired, and matured?

SAFE PEOPLE, SAFE GROUPS (PAGE 281)

We have already seen what safe people ought to look like, but how do we develop relationships with safe people? There are four ways to find such people.

1. *Evaluate and educate your current relationships.* Who among your current circle of friends and acquaintances might be interested in growing deeper in attachment? What step will you take toward finding out?

2. *Seek new relationships.* Which of your current friends and acquaintances do you suspect are not willing or able to handle helping you grow? (Be sure to confirm that before you write them off.) Where might you go to find accepting, forgiving, gracious, and truthful friends who want to promote mutual growth? For ideas, move on to point 3.

3. *Join an organized, relationally focused group.* Look for a support group, a small-group fellowship focusing on intimacy, or a therapy group that has as its primary goal the growth of the individual toward closeness within the group. Such a group will provide a good place to grow out of sinful hiding patterns, harmful self-protective behaviors, or deep hurts and immaturities. Check out local churches. Seek out a Christian counselor or therapist who can recommend a safe place to grow.

4. *Be willing to make economically disadvantageous decisions to find closeness.* Even though it may mean paying a high price (even moving to an area in which genuine relationships can be cultivated), it is an urgent necessity to find a safe place to repair your injured parts and grow. Make this possible economic cost a matter of prayer.

EXCHANGING HIDING FOR RELATIONSHIP (PAGE 283)

Remember the contest between the Sun and the Wind? When we are attacked because of our hiding patterns—by others or ourselves—we simply hold them more tightly. It takes the warm light of grace and safety, with noncritical truthfulness, to help us outgrow our concealments.

- What encouragement about outgrowing your defenses did you find in the story of the child and his security blanket?

- Review how Jenny came out of hiding (pages 285–87 of the text). What does this story tell you about yourself? What will be required of you on your healing journey? And what can you hope for?

A life dedicated to self-protection and hiding can be exchanged for a life full of love, meaningful accomplishments, acceptance, and direction. God wants us, like Jenny, to find a safe place to learn the ways we hide from love. In that place, we are destined to begin the often exciting, often painful work of resolving our hiding patterns, meeting our undeveloped needs, and moving further into Christlikeness.

- Explain "Our redemption is accomplished as we hide *in* God rather than hide *from* him." Give specific details about what it looks like to hide *in* God.

It is, after all, God's love that comes looking for us in our secret hideouts. Thus, my prayer for you is that as you turn away from the dark places of your own shame, fears, and anxieties, you will look first at the kind face of an Officer Josef whom God has provided to help you to safety and growth. May you find God and others walking with you as you come out of hiding!

Coming Out of Hiding

1. What growth in yourself have you sensed since starting this study on hiding from love? What encouragement and help have you found along the way?

2. How has this study affected your relationship with God? your feelings about yourself? your relationships with other people?

3. Begin by thanking God for the progress you just noted—for the growth, the encouragement, the hope, and the healing of relationships you have already experienced—and for what you have learned about hiding from love. Ask him to provide you with the discernment, strength, courage, and support you need to continue along the path of healing toward the restoration of your injured parts. As you continue your journey out of hiding, may you find God and others walking with you.

Now to him who is able to do immeasurably more than all we ask
or imagine, according to his power that is at work within us,
to him be glory in the church and in Christ Jesus throughout
all generations, for ever and ever! Amen.

Ephesians 3:20–21

For information about Dr. Townsend's books, tapes, resources, and speaking engagements, contact

Cloud-Townsend Resources
3176 Pullman Avenue, Suite 104
Costa Mesa, CA 92626
Telephone: 1-800-676-HOPE (4673)
Fax: 1-714-979-7553
email: web@cloudtownsend.com
Web: www.cloudtownsend.com

We want to hear from you. Please send your comments about this
book to us in care of the address below. Thank you.

GRAND RAPIDS, MICHIGAN 49530
www.zondervan.com